ISLAM FOR BEGINNERS

MIRZA YAWAR BAIG

Text copyright © Mirza Yawar Baig 2013

Cover photo copyright © Mirza Yawar Baig 2013

This book is sold subject to the condition that it shall not, by way of trade or otherwise, be lent, resold, hired out, or otherwise circulated without prior written consent of Mirza Yawar Baig, in any form of binding or cover other than that in which it is published and without a similar condition including this condition being imposed on the subsequent purchaser and without limiting the rights under copyright reserved above, no part of this publication maybe reproduced, stored in or introduced into a retrieval system or transmitted in any form or by any means (electronic, mechanical, photocopying, recording or otherwise) without the permission of the copyright owner.

Dedication

I dedicate this book to all those, friends and strangers, who asked me about Islam. I dedicate this book to all those who are genuinely in search of the truth, with the dua that Allah☸ may make their search easy and fruitful culminating in them recognizing their Creator, who one day they will meet.

Why this book

It has been said that true bankruptcy is a full belly and an empty soul. Religion must be a matter of conscious choice. Not a matter of accidental birth. Because on it depends our peace of mind, how we view the world, our relationships with others, what choices we make and the results of those choices in this life and the Hereafter. What we choose to believe or reject must be done thoughtfully after due reflection and investigation because our present and our everlasting future both depend on it. It can't be left to incidental following of traditions and customs we don't even know the origin or meanings of, just because our parents or elders used to do them.

One's spiritual journey is as important if not more, as one's journey in this life in terms of one's career or other criteria and so deserves an equal mindshare and effort.

It has long been on my mind to write a small, easy to understand book about Islam for the average non-Muslim who has questions about Islam and Muslims, many of which may be as a result of the prejudiced representation which has become the fashion in the media and elsewhere today. I believe it is therefore necessary to state the facts as they stand and leave it to the reader to draw their own conclusions.

It is not my purpose in this book to convince you one way or the other. Simply to present facts about Islam so that the reality of what Islam is and stands for is before you. The rest is up to you.

I believe that the single biggest source of conflict is bad information. Wrong information about someone or their culture, beliefs and ways which leads us to making assumptions about them that develop into stereotypes. The difficult part is that for most people it is not easy to get good information, firstly because they don't know who to ask and secondly because in the case of some technical or legal matters it is necessary to first have some basic knowledge and understanding of sources, derivative principles and interpretations to understand a particular ruling. Just as one wouldn't be able to understand a medical diagnosis without some basic knowledge of medicine, so also one can't understand a legal ruling (whether it be secular law or theological) without basic knowledge of the legal framework being used.

On the other hand the media in its single minded pursuit of profit irrespective of means or methods uses Islam in particular as a means of attracting attention by sensationalizing everything possible instead of taking a reasoned and rational approach. The result is that the average viewer/reader is left at best bewildered and at worst, forms negative opinions based purely on propaganda masquerading as fact. 'News' today is closer to advertising copy than to the accurate reporting of events.

It is in this context that I decided to write this book.

Over the years many people, friends and strangers, Muslim and non-Muslim, have asked me questions about Islam.

In answering them I tried to do two things:

1. Give evidence for my answers and explanations from the two foundational sources of Islam, the Qur'an and the Sunnah (Hadith)
2. Try to explain in the common person's language giving examples which are modern and easy to understand.

This seems to have worked well and on the suggestion of some of the questioners who found the answers they were looking for, I have tried to put together as many answers as I can in this book. The arrangement of the questions and answers is not sequential and so you can open the book at any point and read. It is not necessary to read it from beginning to end, though I hope you will do so.

It is my purpose to give you accurate information about Islam to the best of my ability without trying to color your judgment or to convince you one way or the other. What conclusions you come to and what decisions you take after reading this, is entirely up to you. I only hope that whatever you decide will be based on good information and not on propaganda.

It is also my intention to encourage people to conduct their own independent research into Islam, its tenets, culture, rules and regulations, permissions and prohibitions, its world view and its understanding of God (Allah).

And very importantly into the life of its central, single most important figure, the Prophet and Messenger Muhammad ﷺ. I hope you will take the time and trouble to distinguish between what Islam ordains and what Muslims in different parts of the world do as a result of their own local cultures and superstitions, whims and fancies, customs and practice. I wish I could say that all Muslims practice Islam in the pure form that Muhammad ﷺ brought. Unfortunately they don't and the results are sadly visible. That is the reason it is essential to distinguish and differentiate between what is Islam and what is local tradition, culture or superstition. I hope that as a result of reading what is in this book, your interest will be piqued to read more and delve deeper into what Islam really is.

I wish you all the best in your quest for knowledge and pray that you are guided to the truth because in the end it is essential that we know what the truth is and that we believe it and prepare for it. It is the nature of reality that it does not depend on belief for its existence and that one day it has to be faced whether we chose to believe in it or not.

M. Yawar Baig

Table of Contents

What do Muslims believe?... 9

What are the pillars of Islam?.. 25

What is permitted and what is prohibited in foods, business and entertainment?... 55

What do we wear?... 59

How do we live with others?... 61

How do we deal with money?... 69

Common questions asked about Islam............................ 77

Glossary of Terms

Rasoolullahﷺ	Muhammad, Messenger of Allah. The Arabic script after the English means: Peace & Blessings be on him
Allahﷻ	The personal name of God. The Arabic script after the English means 'The Glorious
Rabb	Lord, Sustainer, Protector, Provider for all needs: One of the names of Allahﷻ
Aakhira	Hereafter
Ghaib	Unperceivable (wrongly called Unseen)
Jannah	Paradise
Jahannam	Hell fire
Ribâ	Bank Interest and other similar gains
Shari'ah	Islamic Law
Sunnah	Teachings of Muhammadﷺ which is the second source for Islamic Law
Fajr	Dawn prayer
Dhuhr	Mid-day prayer
Asr	Afternoon prayer
Maghrib	Sunset prayer
Isha	Night prayer

Tahajjud	Prayer in the last part of the night, before dawn
Dhikr	Remembering Allahﷻ in any way
Dua	Supplication, personal prayer asking for whatever one wants to ask Allahﷻ
Jibreel	Angel Gabriel
Wahi	Revelation: the Qur'an
Ali bin Abi Talib	Cousin of Muhammadﷺ who the Shia ask for help instead of asking Allahﷻ
Abdul Qadir Jeelani	A scholar from Baghdad who many Sunnis ask for help instead of asking Allahﷻ
Shirk	Polytheism; joining partners with Allahﷻ in his being, work, actions, attributes or power. Or ascribing divinity to anyone or anything other than Allahﷻ
Kufr	Denial of Allahﷻ including denying His attributes, commands, words (Qur'an) or His being (atheism)

What do Muslims believe?

We believe in Allahﷻ

We believe that Allahﷻ is One, alone, without partners, children, family, associates, equals or shareholders; incomparable to and unlike anything in His creation.

We believe that Allahﷻ needs nobody and nothing and that everybody and everything needs Him. We believe that everything and everyone will exist as long as Allahﷻ wishes and ends or dies when He decrees.

We believe that Allahﷻ provides for and sustains everyone and everything and needs nothing from anyone or anything.

We believe that all that exists was created by Allahﷻ as He wished, in the form and nature He wished, at the time and place that He wished, without anyone else's help or support and that He will cause it to end when He wishes without anyone else's help or support.

We believe that Allahﷻ created all that we know and all that we are not yet aware of without getting tired in the least and without needing any rest.

We believe that Allahﷻ does not have and is not limited by our natures and attributes and so our own limitations of strength, intelligence, power, influence, knowledge or energy or anything else don't apply to Him.

We believe that Allahﷻ has His own unique attributes and qualities some of which He told us about.

We believe that though words similar to those we use may be utilized to describe the attributes of Allahﷻ i.e. sight, hearing, mercy, forgiveness, hand, face and so on – none of these can be compared to our attributes. We believe He has these attributes because He mentioned them without wondering about or trying to conceptualize their exact nature. We do this because we believe that the attributes of Allahﷻ, by definition are beyond the comprehension of human intelligence, except that which Allahﷻ chose to explain to us.

Therefore we believe that Allahﷻ alone is worthy of worship and worthy of asking for help and so He alone we worship without associating anyone or anything with Him in any way whatever and He alone we ask for help.

We don't worship anyone other than Allahﷻ, no matter how holy, powerful or wise that individual may have been. So we don't worship Jesus, Moses or Muhammadﷺ or any other prophet. We don't worship any celestial object like the sun or moon or any star or planet or constellation. We don't worship any animal, bird, mountain, river or ocean.

We don't worship anything in creation. All such beliefs are false, not part of Islam and amount to (Shirk) polytheism.

We worship only Allahﷻ, the Creator of them all.

We also don't ask the help of anyone other than Allahﷻ nor do we join anyone with Allahﷻ when we ask for His help. So we don't ask the help of Jesus, Muhammadﷺ, Ali bin Abi Talib, Abdul Qadir Jeelani, any saint, any holy man or woman, any angel, jinn or creature of any kind. All such beliefs are false, not part of Islam and amount to (Shirk) polytheism and place a person outside Islam.

We ask the help only of Allahﷻ, the Creator of them all.

We also don't ascribe the qualities of Allahﷻ to anyone or anything in His creation because He mentioned that nothing in creation resembles Him in any respect. So we don't believe that any human being has or had any divine quality and we don't ascribe any human or other creature quality to Allahﷻ. We don't believe in and refute and deny beliefs that ascribe qualities of knowledge of the future, omnipresence and omniscience, ability to influence the universe or people's lives, interfere in the order and process of the universe and all such things to people; like Jesus, Muhammadﷺ, Ali bin Abi Talib, the Imams of the Shia, Abdul Qadir Jeelani or any other human being, angel, jinn or other creature.

All such beliefs are false, not part of Islam and amount to (Shirk) polytheism and place a person outside Islam.

We believe that Allahﷻ is unlike anything in His creation and is not bound by any of the rules of creation. He makes the rules of creation and as the Rule Maker, He can change any rule He wants, whenever He wants.

This is the core, fundamental theological principle in Islam, called Tawheed – unity of worship of Allahﷻ alone.

Any mixture or adulteration of belief by associating anyone with Allah﷾ either in His worship or by asking the help of anyone else along with or instead of Allah﷾ or of ascribing divinity or divine qualities to anyone other than Allah﷾ to whom alone all divinity and divine qualities belong; renders the individual out of Islam. Similarly denying Allah﷾, His attributes, His Book, His promises, His laws, the meeting with Him, His Messengerﷺ or his teachings also render a person out of Islam.

A Muslim is conscious of Allah﷾ all the time. For example when he meets someone he says, 'As salaamu alaikum' (May peace be on you) which is a dua. When he parts company he says, 'Fee Aman-illah' (may you be in the protection of Allah﷾). When he starts anything, be it a journey or a meal, he says, 'Bismillah' (in the name of Allah﷾). When he ends he says, 'Ahamdulillah' (all praise and thanks are for Allah﷾). He says this also whenever he receives anything good. If he gets any bad news or suffers loss he says, 'Inna lillahi wa inna ilaihi rajioon' (we are from Allah﷾ and to Him is our return). When he faces any difficulty he says, 'HasbiAllah' (Allah﷾ is sufficient for me). When he promises to do something he says, 'Insha'Allah' (If Allah﷾ wills). If he sees anything good he says, Subhan'Allah' (Glorious is Allah﷾) and if he sees or does anything bad he says, 'Astaghfirullah' (I ask the forgiveness of Allah﷾). If he is led astray he says, 'Aaoodhubillah' (I seek the protection of Allah﷾). When he is surprised by the magnitude of something he says, 'Allahu Akbar' (Allah﷾ is the greatest).

Then there are the daily duas (supplications, prayers) that every Muslim child is taught. These are short supplications for goodness, health, protection from evil, asking for ease and increase in sustenance, thankfulness for all the blessings that we have been given. Supplications at the beginning of a journey, while entering the house and while leaving it; before starting a meal and upon ending it; before sleeping and upon waking up; before entering the toilet and when leaving it; when wearing new clothes; when visiting the sick, when condoling someone's death and when congratulating someone. The Muslim does all this and more apart from his formal worship (Salah or Namaz) as a matter of course in his daily life.

This is not an exhaustive list but it demonstrates how the daily language of the Muslim is sprinkled with the remembrance of Allahﷻ so that he is conscious of His Power and Majesty all the time, in every situation.

It would perhaps not be out of place to say that no other people mention God so often and in so many parts of their lives, as do the Muslims. Allahﷻ is very important to Muslims.

Do's	Don'ts
Worship, ask for help and ascribe divine attributes only to Allahﷻ.	Don't worship, don't ask for help and don't ascribe divine attributes to anyone other than Allahﷻ, no matter who that may be.

We believe in the Messengers

We believe that Muhammad ﷺ like all the prophets and messengers before him was a human being; was not divine and was a messenger of Allah ﷻ. We believe in addition that he was the last and final messenger of Allah ﷻ and that there is no prophet or messenger after him. We believe in him and in the message that he brought which is called Islam. Believing in Muhammad ﷺ as the last and final messenger is part of the foundational belief and creed of Islam. We refute and deny anyone who claims Prophethood after Muhammad ﷺ. We reject the claim to Prophethood of Mirza Ghulam Ahmad Qadiyani (followers called Mirzayi, Ahmedi or Qadiyani) or anyone else who came after Muhammad ﷺ and claimed to be a prophet or messenger of Allah ﷻ. We consider all such people to be liars and their claims to be false.

We believe that every messenger of Allah ﷻ brought the same message of Islam and that they were all Muslims – people who submit themselves to Allah ﷻ - and that they also invited their people to submit to Allah ﷻ.

We believe that none of them told their people to worship them instead of Allah ﷻ and so we deny all such beliefs which claim divinity for the messengers of Allah ﷻ; like Jesus, his mother Mary or anyone else. We believe that neither Mary nor Jesus told people that they were divine. Nor did Jesus claim to be the son of Allah ﷻ, nor did Mary call herself, 'Mother of God', nor did either of them tell the people to ask for their help instead of asking for the help of

- Allah☗. Those who claim such things are guilty of fabricating lies about Jesus and Mary and of slander against Jesus and Mary. To accuse a messenger of changing the message is slander and that is what the claims of divinity for Jesus and Mary amount to. Muslims deny all such claims. We believe that Jesus was a messenger of Allah☗, like other messengers before him including Noah, Abraham, Jacob, Joseph, David, Solomon and Moses and like the last messenger who came after him, Muhammad☗. We believe that Jesus preached nothing other than what he had been sent with and that he performed his duty as a messenger of Allah☗ with complete integrity and honesty. We believe that those who claim that he was son-of-god are making a grave allegation against him and will answer to Allah☗ on the Day of Judgment when Jesus himself will refute and deny them.

We believe in all the Messengers of Allah☗ that He mentioned and we believe that He sent messengers to all people in all times. However we don't believe about anyone that he was a messenger of Allah☗ unless he is one of those mentioned by Allah☗. We follow only the message of the last of them, Muhammad☗ because his message supports the truth of all messages that came before it in terms of monotheism and the worship of Allah☗ alone and supercedes and overrides every other message that came before it in terms of the Law. In the words of Muhammad☗, 'If Moses were alive today, he would follow the Law that I have brought.'

Do's	Don'ts
Believe in Muhammad ﷺ as the Prophet and Messenger of Allah ﷻ and His slave and creature.	Not believe that Muhammad ﷺ was other than human. Not believe that anyone else was a prophet or messenger of Allah ﷻ after Muhammad ﷺ

We believe in the Books of Allah ﷻ

We believe that this last message consists of the Qur'an – the Book of Revelation – which is the direct speech of Allah ﷻ and is the primary source of Islamic law and the teachings of Muhammad ﷺ which are an explanation of the Qur'an in terms of its application and practice in daily life.

The latter is known as the Sunnah and is also revelation but of a different kind. The Qur'an is recited in worship and is a part of worship. The Sunnah is studied and applied in life and shows us how to worship; among many other things. However it is not recited in worship as is the Qur'an.

We follow the Qur'an in every word that it contains and accept all its injunctions without hesitation, change, alteration or reservation. We accept all the divine laws it contains without reservation and believe that this Divine Law is the only law that has a right to be implemented on earth. We believe that whoever tries to alter anything of the Qur'an, be it a single letter of it; anyone who denies anything of the Qur'an, be it a single letter of it; anyone who rejects anything of the Qur'an, be it a single letter of it; anyone who makes fun of or doesn't believe in any of the promises, descriptions and narrations of the matters of the Unperceivable and the Hereafter, has left Islam.

We believe that it is essential for the Muslim to believe in, understand and implement the Qur'an and Sunnah in his/her life because this is the best possible way to live.

We believe in all the other Divine Books that Allahﷻ mentioned in the Qur'an i.e. Torah, Zaboor and Injeel – that they were Divine Revelation in their original form. We don't accept the changes that have been made to them and don't accept them as a source of Islamic Law. We believe that the people who made the changes had no right to do so and that they exceeded their authority. To make changes in a Divine Revelation is comparable to making changes in the writing of an author without his permission. We call that 'copyright violation' and it is a cognizable offence. How then can we accept changes in Divine Revelation without the permission of its author, Allahﷻ? That is why no Muslim will ever agree to any change in the Qur'an because she/he understands his own position with respect to Allahﷻ.

We believe that it is essential to understand and implement the Sunnah (teaching, way) of Muhammadﷺ in our lives because the Sunnah explains the Qur'an. As mentioned above, we believe the Sunnah to be another form of Revelation which is called Wahi Ghayr Matlo'o (revelation that is not recited in prayer). We believe that this revelation was sent to explain the Qur'an and so is an essential part of Islamic theology and the second most important source of Islamic Law. We believe that anyone who denies the Sunnah partially or in totality and claims that the Qur'an is sufficient for him, proclaims his own gross ignorance and has left Islam. Even a cursory study of the Qur'an will make it clear to the sincere person that the explanation of the Law is essential to understand and implement the law.

So is the case with the Qur'an and the Sunnah. The Sunnah complements the Qur'an and is essential for one to be able to understand the method of carrying out Qur'anic injunctions and laws. Without the Sunnah it is impossible to implement the Qur'an and therefore those who reject the Sunnah are also rejecting the Qur'an.

Just to give one example, the Qur'an orders the Believer to establish the prayer (Salah) but is silent on the method of prayer. It orders the Believer to pay Zakat (obligatory charity) but is silent on what it is to be paid on and its value. Both of these and numerous such matters were explained by Muhammadﷺ by means of the revelation he received about these details which we know as the Sunnah.

So one who does not accept the Sunnah can't pray and can't pay Zakat which automatically renders him out of Islam. Finally the Qur'an orders the Believer in more than one place to follow the way of Muhammadﷺ (Sunnah) and so anyone who refuses to accept the Sunnah has denied the order of the Qur'an which places him out of Islam.

Do's	Don'ts
Accept the Qur'an as the final revelation, read it, understand it and implement it in your life. Accept the Sunnah of Muhammad ﷺ and follow it to the best of your ability.	Don't criticize, make fun of, express opinions on and generally speak loosely about the Qur'an or the Sunnah.
Always have and express the highest respect for the Qur'an and Sunnah which the Revelation of the Word of Allah ﷻ and the beautiful teachings of His Messenger ﷺ deserve.	Don't sit with people who make fun of the Qur'an or Sunnah and don't have them as your friends.

We believe in the Angels, Day of Judgment and Destiny

We believe in the angels of Allahﷻ, in general that they are creatures of Allahﷻ which He created to carry out His orders and for other purposes as He wishes. We believe specifically in those He named, i.e. Jibreel (Gabriel), Mika'eel, Israfeel, Maalik (angel in charge of Jahannam), Ridhwaan (angel in charge of Jannah) and Malak-ul-Mawth (Angel of Death).

We believe in Jannah (Paradise) and Jahannam (Hell) and in all the details of both that Allahﷻ mentioned in the Qur'an and that His Messengerﷺ mentioned in his teachings (Sunnah).

We believe in the Yawn ul Aakhira, also called Yawm ul Qiyaama (Day of Judgment), Al Meezaan (the Scale on which the deeds of people will be weighed), Al Qalam (the Pen), Al Lawh ul Mahfooz (the Sacred, Protected Tablet), Al Arsh (the Throne of Allahﷻ) and Al Kursi (the Footstool), As-Siraat (the bridge over Jahannam – Hell), the Hawdh ul Kauthar (the pool of Muhammadﷺ) and all other such matters of Al-Ghaib (Unperceivable) which Allahﷻ mentioned in the Qur'an or which His Messengerﷺ told us about. We believe in all of them without asking 'How' – without asking about their specific nature and quality. We believe that they are as Allahﷻ and His Messengerﷺ described them and that it is not necessary or possible for the human being to know more or to try to encompass of the knowledge of Allahﷻ more than He wishes.

So we believe in all these things absolutely and without doubt to the extent that we have been informed and don't extend our own explanations or interpretations about what has been described. Nor do we deny anything of what has been described. It is this obedience that is the hallmark of the Muslim and we exhibit this obedience.

We believe in destiny; that Allahﷻ has decreed for us matters which are not in our control e.g. our death, illness, health, our sustenance (including material wealth). We believe that whatever Allahﷻ has decreed will come to pass and that we have no control over it. We believe also that there are things about our lives that Allahﷻ has given into our control e.g. the sources of our earning and spending, how we live, what we eat, how we treat people, whether or not we fulfill the rights of Allahﷻ and of people and so on; about which we will be questioned and rewarded or punished as the case may deserve.

Our (the Islamic) belief in destiny is not that it is absolute in all respects and that we are compelled by it but that it gives us limited freedom. For example the quantity of our sustenance (Rizq) is fixed but we have the liberty to take it using permitted or prohibited means. Each choice has its own consequences. We are free to choose but the choice is not free. Every choice has a consequence in this world and a reward or punishment in the Hereafter associated with it.

The means don't affect the quantity but they will affect what happens to us on the Day of Judgment. In order to save us from the evil consequences of our own deeds, Allahﷻ sent

His Messenger ﷺ and His Revelation (Qur'an) to teach us the right ways. If someone chooses to ignore them and insists on doing whatever he wills without a thought about the consequences of his actions then he will have only himself to blame.

What are the pillars of Islam?

The Pillars of Islam are five:

Shahadatain (Twin Testimonies)

To bear witness that there is nobody worthy of worship except Allahﷻ; to believe this in the heart and to act according to this in all aspects of life (not to worship anyone other than Allahﷻ or ask for help from anyone other than Allahﷻ and not to join anyone with Allahﷻ in anything relating to Him); and to bear witness that Muhammadﷺ is the messenger of Allahﷻ and is His last and final messenger.

These two aspects of bearing witness are essential for one to enter Islam. If one does this i.e. believes the above and says it out aloud if they can (even if he/she does it on their own), then they are Muslim and have entered Islam.

Normally it is customary to accept Islam in the presence of witnesses as that is more supportive and you get the blessings of others. But it is not a requirement for entering Islam. Allahﷻ is enough as a witness and so if one wants to enter Islam there is nothing that needs to delay that action especially since dying without Islam leads to the Hellfire. Since Islam is the original religion of all people and all people are born on Islam, when someone enters Islam we don't call them 'convert' but we call them 'revert' because they have in effect reverted to their own original state.

Salah

Salah is the name for the formal prayer in Islam which Muslims perform five times daily. Fajr is performed at dawn, Dhuhr is a noon prayer, Asr is performed in the afternoon, Maghrib is the sunset prayer, and Isha is the night prayer.

Salah is a pillar of Islam and something which indicates that a person is Muslim. Salah is the proof that one has entered Islam. It is the physical manifestation by action of the faith that a Muslim has in his heart that he worships nobody except Allahﷻ. Once he has that faith, he demonstrates it by actually worshipping Allahﷻ in the way that Allahﷻ prescribed and taught His Messengerﷺ. If one says that nobody is worthy of worship except Allahﷻ (La ilaaha ill-Allah) but then does not actually worship Allahﷻ, then how can he say that he has faith? That is why leaving Salah negates Islam and places a person outside Islam.

Salah is a gift from Allahﷻ and is the means for the Muslim to connect to his Rabb (Creator, Sustainer, Maintainer, Protector, fulfiller of all needs). It is the highest and most powerful of means; the most potent tool that a Believer has to invoke for anything that he needs in life. It is his 'charge' of energy which gives him a special light and power all through his days in this life and is a light in his grave and deliverance in Al-Aakhira. More about the Salah later because it is such an important part of this Deen.

Sawm (fasting)

Fasting is an obligatory act during the month of Ramadan. Muslims must abstain from food, drink, and sexual intercourse from dawn to dusk during this month, and be especially mindful of other sins. Fasting is obligatory for every Muslim over the age of puberty.

The fast is meant to allow Muslims to seek nearness to Allahﷻ, to express their gratitude to and dependence on Him, atone for their past sins, and to remind them of the Hereafter. Fasting is meant for us to reflect on our lives, straighten our actions and bring them in line with the commands of Allahﷻ. Fasting reinforces obedience to Allahﷻ in all things without exception; that we obey Him whether or not the command is likable, logical or not. Fasting in Ramadan is like an annual retreat and intensive training program in obedience to Allahﷻ. It is an opportunity to repent our sins and transform our lives.

Fasting during Ramadan is obligatory, but for several groups for whom it would be inadvisable for health reasons or excessively problematic; e.g. young children, diabetics, elderly people, and pregnant or nursing mothers, it is acceptable not to fast and they can make up their missed fasts or pay for someone else's food. The specific details of what is to be done in each case must be ascertained depending on specific circumstances. Fasting is a means of gaining Allahﷻ's pleasure and so is something that every Muslim looks forward to doing.

Ramadan is awaited and Muslims rejoice when it comes because it brings with it special rewards and blessings.

Zakat

Zakat is charity which is obligatory for anyone who is able to give it – based on a specific amount of wealth that one has accumulated for 12 months. Zakat is a personal responsibility of every Muslim who has the minimum amount of wealth that makes him liable to pay Zakat. Zakat is the purification of wealth just as prayer is purification of the body and heart. Islam makes charity not only an act of goodness but an act which is compulsory and punishable if not done.

In general terms Zakat consists of spending 2.5% of one's wealth for the benefit of the poor or needy, including family, strangers, debtors and travelers. Different percentages of Zakat are payable for agricultural income, sale goods and so on and it is necessary to find out how much is due based on individual circumstances. Zakat is also permitted to be spent for the benefit of needy non-Muslims and where there is an accumulation of it, for the construction or maintenance of facilities for common good, like schools, hospitals and so on. Muslims are also highly encouraged to spend more over and above Zakat as an act of voluntary charity (Sadaqa), to achieve additional divine reward. Anyone who refuses to pay Zakat after being eligible for it, or who denies that Zakat is compulsory has left Islam.

Hajj

Hajj is the pilgrimage to the Ka'aba – located in the Grand Mosque in Makkah. Every able bodied Muslim, man or woman is obliged to make this pilgrimage at least once in their lifetime, if they have the means (financial, health, safety) to do so.

The Hajj consists of rituals that recreate the epic journey and sacrifice of Prophet Ibrahim ﷺ and his family which Allah ﷻ liked so much that He prescribed them as acts of worship for His Messenger Muhammad ﷺ and his people. The Hajj underlines the fact that all virtue in Islam is the obedience of Allah ﷻ whether or not that action in itself, 'makes sense' in our modern context. Similarly all vice is disobedience of Allah ﷻ no matter what modern society may choose to think of such acts in today's world and environment. This is a very important underlying principle of Islam which means 'submission'.

Hajj like, the Sajda (prostration) in Salah reaffirms the submission of the Muslim to His Rabb and his commitment to obey Him above all else and irrespective of whether that obedience is approved by people or not. The Hajj is a truly international, multicultural, multiracial, multiethnic gathering which represents the global nature of the Muslims and reiterates the brotherhood of faith, based on submission to Allah ﷻ. It is a gathering of Muslims from all corners of the globe only for the worship of Allah ﷻ and to renew their brotherhood of faith that transcends all boundaries.

Before I end this chapter, I want to share with you a beautiful Hadith of Rasoolullahﷺ when the angel Jibreel۩ came in the form of a man and had a conversation with him. I want to share this with you because it illustrates the divine nature of this Deen and covers all essential matters of our creed and belief. The companions of Rasoolullahﷺ (his Sahaba) saw him and Umar ibn Al Khattab؄ narrated the incident. What days were those when men saw the angels and Jibreel۩ who is himself a messenger of Allahﷻ, visited Muhammad, the Messengerﷺ of Allahﷻ.

Narrated Umar ibn Al Khattab؄

While we were sitting with the Messenger of Allah, peace and blessings of Allah upon him, one day, there appeared before us a man dressed in extremely white clothes and with very black hair. No traces of travel were visible on him, and none of us knew him.

He sat down close by the Prophet, peace and blessings upon him, rested his knees against his knees and placed his palms on his thighs, and said, O Muhammad! Inform me about Islam." We were very surprised at this behavior. Muhammadﷺ said, "Islam is that you should testify that there is no deity save Allah and that Muhammad is His Messenger, that you should perform Salah (ritual prayer), pay the Zakat (compulsory charity), fast during Ramadan, and perform Hajj (pilgrimage) to the House (the Ka'aba at Makkah), if you can find a way to it (find the means for making the journey to it)."

Said he (the man), "You have spoken truly." We were astonished at his thus questioning him and telling him that he was right, but he went on to say, "Inform me about Imaan (faith)." He (the Messenger of Allah) answered, "It is that you believe in Allah and His angels and His Books and His Messengers and in the Last Day, and in fate (Qadr), both in its good and in its evil aspects."

He said, "You have spoken truly." Then he (the man) said, "Inform me about Ihsan." He (the Messenger of Allah) answered, "It is that you should worship Allah as though you could see Him, for though you cannot see Him, yet He sees you."

He said, "Inform me about the Hour." He (the Messenger of Allah) said, "About that, the one questioned knows no more than the questioner." So he said, "Well, inform me about the signs thereof (of its coming)." Said he, "They are, that the slave-girl will give birth to her mistress, that you will see the barefooted ones, the naked, the destitute, the herdsmen of sheep (competing with each other) in raising lofty buildings."

Thereupon the man went off. I waited a while, and then he (the Messenger of Allah) said, "O 'Umar, do you know who that questioner was?"

I replied, "Allah and His Messenger know better." He said, "That was Jibreel. He came to teach you your religion."

Blessed are we to have a Divine religion to follow. Not something that we invented or which was invented by any man, no matter how clever. A religion that has the sanction of Allahﷻ himself, brought down by his powerful messenger Jibreelﷺ and taught to us by Muhammadﷺ our master, teacher, supreme leader and the one who we follow in all respects.

There are two kinds of knowledge that are available to humankind.
1. Knowledge that we gain by exploration, experimentation & testing, deductive reasoning, logical argument and all other such means.
2. Knowledge gained from listening to the voice of the Creator when He speaks to us, which we call the Revelation. The last of these Revelations is the Qur'an, which Allahﷻ revealed to His last and final Messenger, Muhammad (Peace and Blessings be upon him and all other Messengers who came before him).

The essential difference between the two bodies of knowledge is that the second one begins where the first one ends. Islam invites the researcher towards the humility of real learning by acknowledging that his own efforts can take him only thus far and that beyond that frontier he needs the help of his Creator to know more.

The Qur'an is the Revealed Word of Allahﷻ. It is His Speech. It is He, as our Creator, Sustainer, Provider of every need, the One we worship alone without ascribing any partners, helpers, assistants or relatives and the One to whom we will all return on the Day of Judgment; who is speaking to us through His Messenger, Muhammadﷺ to whom the Qur'an was revealed. As such the Qur'an is perfection itself; based on the logic that there can never be anything devised or created by humans that can exceed in beauty, insight, power or truth, the Word of Allahﷻ Himself.

The wisdom of the Creator can never be less than the wisdom of His Creatures.

Just like a computer, no matter how complex and powerful can never exceed the power and intelligence of its maker, so also the wisdom of a human being, no matter who he or she is, can never exceed the wisdom and knowledge of his own Creator. Whether he accepts the Creator or not, does not matter because a fact does not change because you refuse to accept it.

Introducing any change into the Revelation in the name of 'progress' or 'development', is therefore not acceptable because it is illegal and a violation of copyright (the author did not authorize any changes) and in reality can only be detrimental because logically someone who knows less can't make a progressive change to the writing of someone who knows more. Thus the Revelation, the Qur'an is perfection itself and can't be 'improved' by anyone. The Message has been perfected and completed and no further changes are possible or necessary. It is totally illogical to first accept that the Qur'an is in fact the Word of Allahﷻ and then to say that it needs to be changed because it is not relevant any longer.

Muslims believe that the Qur'an can never become out of date for the simple reason that its author is Allahﷻ himself who created the world and then sent His Messengerﷺ with instructions of how to live in it.

Allahﷻ stated categorically:

Ma'aida: 5:3 *Today have I perfected for you your religion, and have completed upon you the full measure of My blessings, and have chosen Islam for you as your religion.*

Therefore Islam does not need to be reinterpreted or altered to suit any new situation. Islam is not a philosophy or system of blind faith, superstition, mythology or cultural rituals, which need constant reinterpretation and readjustment to be aligned to new emerging facts.
Islam is the result of the Revelation of knowledge from the Creator, so all facts, if indeed they are facts, will automatically be aligned to the Revelation. Islam is therefore not only, not in danger from any new discoveries in any branch of science but welcomes all such research and waits to welcome the researchers into its fold as they stand there marveling at the creation, aware of their own insignificance. If they are people of integrity then they have no alternative but to acknowledge and bow down before the Creator and to worship Him alone. Allahﷻ challenges all intelligent people, particularly all scientists and researchers to think and use their reason:

Fussilat 41:53 *Verily We will show them Our signs in the utmost horizons [of the universe] and within themselves, so that it will become clear to them that this [Qur'an] is indeed the truth. Is it not enough [for them to know] that your Rabb is witness unto everything?*

All discoveries, realizations and understanding about the universe can only confirm and reinforce the message of the Qur'an. If they don't then it means that the discovery is faulty and needs to be checked again. The discovery does not 'prove' the authenticity of the Qur'an; the Qur'an proves the authenticity of the discovery. Islam therefore welcomes all research to gain more understanding of ourselves and our nature and of the universe in which we live, because these discoveries can only bring the researcher closer to Allahﷻ and to the point where he/she will acknowledge and worship the one who created him.

Allahﷻ mentions this clearly and encourages scientific research, the result of which Allahﷻ promises will be an understanding of where we stand in terms of ourselves and our Creator and our responsibility to Him as well as to each other on this earth. It is when research is done with sincerity and the genuine desire to learn, that true realization about ourselves and our world happens.

A'al Imraan 3:190 *Verily, in the creation of the heavens and the earth, and in the succession of night and day, there are indeed messages for people of intelligence, [They are those] who remember Allah, standing sitting and lying on their sides and reflect on (research into) the creation of the heavens and the earth (and spontaneously cry out): "O our Rabb! You have not created [any of] this without meaning and purpose. Limitless are You in your glory! Keep us safe, from the punishment of the Fire.*

Islam means submission so when a Muslim writes about Islam he does so from that perspective.
This is often the most difficult step to take; to submit ourselves, our likes and dislikes, our will, our feelings and emotions, thoughts and logic to the will of Allahﷻ.

Submit unquestioningly and with complete acceptance and trust that His way is the best and in following it lays our own success in this world and the next.

Islam invites the person to reflect, that though a seatbelt restricts movement, it is precisely this restriction that is the means of saving life. The one who recognizes the value of the 'restriction' actually welcomes it and invites others to wear seatbelts. So also in Islam, the Muslim recognizes that in submitting to the 'restrictions and rules' of Islam lies his own benefit in this world and deliverance in the Aakhira. The one who wants freedom from seatbelts is opening himself to grievous injury, even death in the event of a crash, so also someone who refuses to recognize Allahﷻ is opening himself to the embarrassment of facing Him on the Day of Judgment and realizing too late that what he had been told all through his life in the world was not fantasy or imaginary but fact. That is why Islam emphasizes submission to such an extent that even worship is to be done in a prescribed manner. One can't worship Allahﷻ in any way that one may wish.
One has to do it in the way shown to Rasoolullahﷺ by Allahﷻ and by Rasoolullahﷺ to us. Any worship that is done without following the prescribed way is not

acceptable. Naturally the same principle of submission extends to every single aspect of life, both private and public. Islam is not about our private space alone. It is about our public life, about our relations with society, our dealings, manners, legal framework and government.

This is logical because Allahﷻ's instructions naturally must extend to all aspects of life and cannot be restricted to some rituals of worship alone. Islam prescribes what is good for all of society, Muslim or not and prohibits what is bad for all of society. Islam is not for Muslims alone. It is for all of humankind, for their benefit in this world and their everlasting success in the Hereafter. Islam is the way which when followed with sincerity, leads to the creation of a society that is based on non-discrimination, equality before the law, universal justice, compassion and concern for one another; support for the weak, controls on the strong. A society that is based on timeless ethical and moral values that place the good of the many, over personal freedom to indulge oneself. Its punishments favor the innocent victim of crime over the criminal and it results in peace, safety and harmony for all people, Muslim or not.

Salah (It's outer and inner reality)

Salah is so important that I decided that I would dedicate a special section to it so that we can understand its true importance and what a great asset it is. This is essential if we are to use it as it is meant to be used, as the supreme resource in all respects, as a means of seeking closeness to Allahﷻ, seeking His favor, seeking His help in all matters of this life and seeking His forgiveness on the Day of Judgment.

Salah is the name for the formal prayer in Islam. It is a pillar of Islam and something which indicates that a person is Muslim. It is an accepted principle in Islamic Law that the one who doesn't establish Salah, i.e. doesn't pray, has ceased to be a Muslim.

14 centuries ago an incident happened that had never happened before. Muhammadﷺ the Messenger of Allahﷻ was taken on a multidimensional tour of the universe by His Rabb defying all laws of physics. That is because the One who makes the rules is not bound by them. About this journey which Allahﷻ took his last and final Messengerﷺ on, He said:

Isra 17: 1. *Glorified (and Exalted) is He (Allah) [above all that (evil) they associate with Him] Who took His slave (Muhammadﷺ) for a journey by night from Al-Masjid-al-Haram (at Makkah) to the farthest mosque (in Jerusalem), the neighborhood of which We have blessed, in order that We might show him (Muhammadﷺ) of Our Ayat (signs). Verily, He is the All-Hearer, the All-Seer.*

On this journey Rasoolullahﷺ was taken from one dimension into another, one heaven into another and then onwards to see wherever His Rabb willed. And there, his Rabb gave him a gift. A gift that was not only for him but by his Baraka (blessing) a gift for his entire Ummah (followers, Muslims) because this Ummah was to be given a special responsibility. This Ummah that was created to do the work of the Anbiya (prophets) because their Nabi was the final Nabi (prophet). Allahﷻ stopped Nubuwwat (Prophethood) and Risaalat (Messengership) but the work of Nubuwwat and Risaalat had to continue until the Day of Judgment because people of all times need to be introduced to their Rabb and need guidance with respect to their lives.

It was therefore necessary that this Ummah be given the means of coming into the presence of their Rabb whose work they were doing to ask for His help and to connect with Him to draw strength and inspiration. Salah is this link that links the Rabb (Allahﷻ) to his slaves and enables the slave to invoke the power of his Creator whenever he needs to do so. Salah is our single biggest need in our lives.

Salah is the proof that one has entered Islam. It is the physical manifestation by action of the faith that a Muslim has in his heart that he worships nobody except Allahﷻ. Once he has that faith, he demonstrates it by actually worshipping Allahﷻ in the way that Allahﷻ prescribed and taught His Messengerﷺ. Salah is a matter of great seriousness and consequence; an indicator of a person being a Muslim or not.

If one says that nobody is worthy of worship except Allahﷻ (La ilaaha ill-Allah) but then does not actually worship Allahﷻ, then how can he say that he has faith? Salah is the action which distinguishes and sets apart the Believer from the non-Believer. The Believer prays and the non-believer doesn't. It is that simple. The prayer is the criterion and by our action – of praying or not praying – we pass judgment on ourselves.

The Salah is the means for the Muslim to connect to his Rabb (Creator, Sustainer, Maintainer, Protector, fulfiller of all needs). It is the highest and most powerful of means; the most potent tool that a Believer has to invoke for anything that he needs in life. It is his 'charge' of energy which gives him a special light and power all through his days in this life and is a light in his grave and deliverance in Al-Aakhira. Allahﷻ ordered His Messengerﷺ to rise and pray and draw the energy for his work from Salah.

Allahﷻ mentioned this when He said to His Nabiﷺ:

Muzammil **73:1.** *O you wrapped in garments (Muhammadﷺ)!* **2.** *Stand (to pray) all night, except a little.* **3.** *Half of it, or a little less than that,* **4.** *Or a little more; and recite the Qur'an (aloud) in a slow, (pleasant tone and) style.* **5.** *Verily, We shall send down to you a weighty Word (the Revelation.).* **6.** *Verily, the rising by night (for Tahajjud prayer) is very hard and most potent and good for governing (the soul), and most suitable for (understanding) the Word (of Allah).*

Allah☬ tells us that we need to connect to Him and draw our spiritual sustenance from that connection if we want to do His work. Salah is our connection to Allah☬. As with all connections we need to examine its quality and improve it if we want to get a response. Allah☬ responded to His Nabi ﷺ and those who prayed and said:

Muzammil 73:20. *Verily, your Lord knows that you do stand (to pray at night) a little less than two-thirds of the night, or half the night, or a third of the night, and so do a party of those with you, And Allah measures the night and the day. He knows that you are unable to pray the whole night, so He has turned to you (in mercy). So, recite you of the Qur'an as much as may be easy for you. He knows that there will be some among you sick, others travelling through the land, seeking of Allah's Bounty; yet others fighting in Allah's Cause. So recite as much of the Qur'an as may be easy (for you), and perform As-Salat (Iqamat-as-Salat) and give Zakat, and lend to Allah a goodly loan, and whatever good you send before you for yourselves, (Nawafil), you will certainly find it with Allah, better and greater in reward. And seek Forgiveness of Allah. Verily, Allah is Oft-Forgiving, Most-Merciful.*

Allah☬ said that He has prepared a special reward for those who pray Tahajjud. He said:

Sajda 32:16. *Their sides forsake their beds, to invoke their Rabb in fear and hope, and they spend (charity in Allah's Cause) out of what We have bestowed on them.* **17.** *No person knows what is kept hidden for them of joy as a reward for what they used to do.*

Salah is to inculcate in the Muslims the habit of asking only from Allahﷻ and bowing only to Him. It is to inculcate in them the discipline of cleansing themselves from impurity and sin, repenting their sins, returning to Allahﷻ, planning their lives, having a timetable, following a leader, standing shoulder to shoulder with their brothers and collectively demonstrating their brotherhood of faith. It is important to understand the benefits of Salah and to realize what a big honor it is so that we gladly and eagerly fulfill its responsibility and benefit from its power.

Allahﷻ used Salah as the means of joining Muslims as brothers with worshipping Him as the criterion of brotherhood. He said:

Anbiya 21:92. *Truly! This, your Ummah [Islamic brotherhood] is one Ummah, and I am your Rabb, therefore worship Me (Alone).*

That is why when Rasoolullahﷺ was asked who a Muslim was, he replied, 'Anyone who believes in La Ilaha Ill-Allahu Muhammadar Rasoolullahi, prays towards our Qibla and eats what we slaughter.' Notice please that he didn't add any of the conditions that we consider necessary today before we are willing to consider another Muslim as our brother. Salah is the action which creates and keeps the Ummah together. The one who doesn't pray with us is not from us. Salah makes us Muslim and it makes us an Ummati (follower) of Rasoolullahﷺ. Our Salah is unique in that it is the only form of worship of any religion which is constant in the main in every place on earth.

Apart from the minor differences of the different Madhaahib (schools of jurisprudence), the Salah in its form, both internal and external is the same for anyone who is Muslim, no matter where he or she lives. It is because Muslims today don't understand the value of Salah that they neglect it and don't realize that their problems and fears are a result of this neglect. Many Muslims, who pray, do it as if discharging a burden instead of recognizing it as a huge gift, benefit and their source of power. They don't look forward to it. They perform it as quickly as they can eager to get out of the Mercy and Grace of Allahﷻ. Sounds strange when I put it like this, but what else would you call our unseemly haste in finishing our Salah and leaving the masjid – if we indeed pray in the masjid in the first place.

Muslims today don't realize that Salah is the answer to their problems in this life and a means of their deliverance from the Hellfire. If they paid attention to Salah and worked to improve its quality then it would become the means of eradicating all fear, anxiety and worry from their lives and the means of invoking the help of Allahﷻ for them. That is what the Salah is for. That is why Salah is so important in Islam that if anyone denies it by word or action (deliberately not praying), then he is in effect denying his own Imaan and so he exits Islam.

The purpose of Salah is to inculcate this basic realization that we worship a living god who sees, hears and is aware of all that we say and do whether it is visible to people or not.

It is meant to remind us five times a day that Allahﷻ is aware of our intentions, speech and actions and that to Him is our return. It is to remind us that the only one we need to fear to displease and to obey without question is Allahﷻ. Only He will call us to account and only to Him we answer.

The Salah is the way that Allahﷻ prefers to be worshipped. He taught it to His Messengerﷺ and from him we learnt how to do it when he said, 'Pray as you see me pray.' This also establishes the importance of the Messengerﷺ in Islam and of obeying him in all that we do. If we have to obey him in the most cardinal of rules – worship – then how can anyone deny obeying him in lesser matters of this worldly life? Those who deny the Sunnah must reflect on this. The same is true of Hajj and all other Faraa'idh of Islam. Allahﷻ ordered them and Rasoolullahﷺ taught us how to implement that order. Without the Sunnah the Qur'an can't be practiced and Islam will cease to exist as a way of life. That is the real motive of those who deny the Sunnah – try to destroy Islam itself. But they forget that they are challenging Allahﷻ himself when they take this route.

Salah is a pillar of Islam. If someone doesn't perform it without a reason valid in the Shari'ah, he has left Islam.

Jabir؞ reports that Rasoolullahﷺ said, *'Between a person and disbelief is discarding prayer.'* (Related by Ahmad, Muslim, Abu Dawud, at-Tirmidhi and Ibn Majah.)

Buraidah؞ reported that Rasoolullahﷺ said, *'The pact between us and them is prayer. Whoever abandons it is a disbeliever.'* (Related by Ahmad, Abu Dawud, at-Tirmidhi, an-Nasa'i and Ibn Majah.)

It sounds strange to us when we hear how Rasoolullahﷺ used to wait for the Salah and used to say to his Muezzin, Sayyidina Bilal﷜: 'Call the Adhaan O Bilal and provide for the coolness of our eyes.' Is the Salah the coolness of our eyes today? And if not, let us seriously ask, 'Why not?' The same behavior is reported from the Companions (Sahaba) of Rasoolullahﷺ who would wait from one Salah to another and would recite the Qur'an in the interim. They were people who were connected with Allahﷻ always. That was the secret of their success whereby in one generation they became the standard for the rest of the world.

It is best to learn how to pray from another person so I would encourage you to do that. There is no shortage of people who know what to do and how to do it and so please learn from them. There are also excellent descriptions of the Salah of Rasoolullahﷺ which it is a good idea to read and correct our own Salah to conform to his. It is only his Salah which is the standard and so we need to ensure that our own conforms to that standard if we want it to be accepted.

It must be remembered that there are three aspects of Salah; all equally important. The first is the external aspect which starts with purification (Tahara) and extends to all the physical actions and recitation of the Qur'an.

The second is the internal aspect which starts with making the intention to pray and extends to all internal aspects of attention, concentration, dedication, understanding, awareness, responding and feeling the presence of Allahﷻ in whose presence we stand when we are in Salah.

The third is the aspect of what the Believer does when he/she completes Salah. It refers to their attitude, behavior, relationships, transactions, society and life once they have come out of Salah. It refers to the changes that can and must come about as a result of having prayed. We will look at each of them in detail.

Pre-Salah: This starts with remembering Allahﷻ often as we go about our daily lives; to make Dhikr of Allahﷻ. And to ensure that our lives are free from sin. To guard our eyes and ears from that which Allahﷻ has prohibited. All of these things affect the Salah of the person because Shaytaan uses these sins and the pictures and sounds of the Haraam to disturb our Salah and to put Wasaawis (evil thoughts) in our minds as we pray. The next step is purification (Tahara) of the body, clothes and place of prayer. It is essential to pay attention to this aspect because depending on the nature of the impurity, it can make the Salah defective or even invalidate it. It is not my intention to go into the details of all the rules of Tahara here but I advise you to please consult people of knowledge and learn the rules of Tahara to ascertain that your Tahara is perfect. Clean clothes, perfume, covering the head – all add to the quality of Salah.

The next aspect is to purify the intention and cleanse it from all forms of evil of Riya (showing others). Then ask for the protection of Allahﷻ from Shaytaan because only Allahﷻ

can protect us from Shaytaan. It is a good idea to read Sura An-Naas before you make Takbeer as it is protection from Wasaawis (whispering of Shaytaan). Focus attention on where you are standing (in the presence of Allahﷻ), free yourself from all worldly thoughts and then make your Niyyah. Remember the words of Ibrahim﷋ which Allahﷻ narrated to us, when he said:

An'aam 6:79. Verily, I have turned my face towards Him Who has created the heavens and the earth Hanifa (worshipping Allah Alone) and I am not of Al-Mushrikun

Stop for a minute and realize what you are saying – in whose presence you are standing. Remind yourself that this may be your last Salah and so make it your best, yet.

The place for the Niyyah (intention) is in the heart and it need not be spoken aloud. Then make Takbeer Tahreema (the first Takbeer with which we enter Salah). Remember that it is called Takbeer Tahreema because it makes everything else, every other action, every other person or concern Haraam. When we stand before Allahﷻ and say Allahu Akbar, we are saying, 'I have cut myself off from everything in this world and have entered the special presence of Allahﷻ.' So how can we allow any thought that refers to anyone other than Allahﷻ to contaminate our communication with our Rabb?

In Salah: Allahﷻ said about the state of Salah:

Mu'minoon 23:1-2 Successful indeed are the believers. 2. Those who pray with concentration and dedication (submissiveness, awareness of Allahﷻ)

The quality of Salah is essential for us to work on. Like anything else, its efficacy depends on its quality. Salah of poor quality is not accepted by Allahﷻ. He said:

Ma'oon 107:4. So woe unto those who pray (hypocrites), 5. Who delay their Salat (prayer) from their stated fixed times, 6. Those who do good deeds only to be seen (by people)

In Salah there is an external aspect which must be adhered to scrupulously. This consists of but is not restricted to:

1. Wearing clean clothes
2. Making all the movements in Salah: Qiyaam, Ruku, Sujood and so on, in an unhurried, deliberate manner ensuring that each is done perfectly.
3. Reciting of the Qur'an as much as one is able in as good a manner as possible.
4. Avoid all unnecessary movement.

The best description of the internal aspect of Salah that I know of, is the answer that Rasoolullahﷺ gave to the Angel Jibreel۝ when he asked the Messengerﷺ, 'Inform me about Al-Ihsaan (excellence).' Rasoolullahﷺ replied, 'It is to worship Allahﷻ as if you can see Him. And though you can't see Him, to know that He can see you.'

We remember when we are praying that Allahﷻ is listening and answering. We know from the Hadith about Sura Al Fatiha that Allahﷻ responds to the slave when he reads Sura Al Fatiha in Salah.

Imam Muslim recorded a Hadith Qudsi narrated by Abu Hurayrah ؓ who reported that Rasoolullahﷺ said,

(Allahﷻ said, 'I have divided the prayer (Al-Fatihah) into two halves between Myself and My slave, and My slave shall have what he asks for.'

When he says, *'All praise and thanks be to Allah, the Lord of existence.'*

Allahﷻ responds and says, 'My slave has praised Me.'

When the slave says, *'The Most Gracious, the Most Merciful.'*

Allah says, 'My slave has glorified Me.'

When he says, *'The Owner of the Day of Recompense.'*

Allah says, 'My slave has related all matters to Me.'

When he says, *'You (alone) we worship, and You (alone) we ask for help.'*

Allah says, 'This is between Me and My slave, and My slave shall acquire what he sought.'

When he says, *'Guide us to the straight path. The way of those on whom You have granted Your grace, not (the way) of those who earned Your anger, nor of those who went astray.'*

Allah says, 'This is for My slave, and My slave shall acquire what he asked for.'

In Salah we recite the speech of Allahﷻ and He listens to it being recited. In Salah we are closest to our Rabb. In Sajda the slave is closest to his Rabb so that is the best time to make dua. Rasoolullahﷺ said to the effect that when a person makes Sajda he is not making that Sajda on the earth but before the Throne of Ar-Rahman. And Allahﷻ said:

Alaq 96:19...   Fall prostrate and draw near to Allah!

Salah is the means of gaining closeness to Allahﷻ and once we have that, what else do we need?

Post: Salah: **'Salah starts when you leave the masjid.' ~Ml. Yunus Patel:**

Our teacher, the great scholar from South Africa, Ml. Yunus Patel (RA) used to say, 'Salah starts when you leave the masjid.' He meant that we need to live our lives in obedience to Allahﷻ and to the Sunnah of His Messengerﷺ. In Salah we asked Allahﷻ to guide us to the Straight Path – the path of His Messengerﷺ. So how can we leave Salah and deny that path and follow someone else's path?

Ibn Al-Qayyim ® said, 'Salah (al-Fatiha) is Tawba (repentance). When the slave says, 'Not from those who incurred your anger or from those who are misguided'; he makes Tawba (repents) from all actions leading to the anger of Allahﷻ and all actions of misguidance.

How do we know if our Salah is good and if we are living our Salah? Allahﷻ said:

Ankabut 29:45. *Recite (O Muhammadﷺ) what has been revealed to you of the Book (the Qur'an), and establish As-Salat. Verily, As-Salat (the prayer) prevents from Al-Fahsha' (sins of shamelessness) and Al-Munkar (sins of disbelief & rebellion) and the remembering of (you by) Allah (in front of the angels) is greater [than your remembering Allah]. And Allah knows what you do.*

So when we are engaged in our worldly affairs and find that we are still drawn to sin, then we must examine the quality of our Salah. There is the story of the person who they complained to Rasoolullahﷺ about saying that he used to commit all kinds of sin. He asked them if he prayed. They said that he did pray. Rasoolullahﷺ said, 'Tell him to continue to pray.' The point here is that if the Salah is good then it will make us ashamed of committing sin. How can we disobey Allahﷻ, indulge in Haraam and then stand before Him if our Salah has any meaning in it at all?

This is not to give the impression that it is acceptable to commit sin as long as one is praying. May Allahﷻ protect us from the Shaytaan's way of deriving wrong meanings from things.

Finally Allahﷻ told us that He will test us in this life and to take the help of Salah when that happens. He said:

Baqara 2:45 *Seek help in patience and Salah*

Baqara 2: 153. *O you who believe! Seek help in patience and As-Salat. Truly! Allah is with As-Sabirin (the patient).*

Salah is the biggest and most powerful resource of the Muslim. It is his weapon against all enemies. It is his greatest pleasure to be with His Rabb. It is what he finds peace, solace and comfort in. It is his refuge and a place of tranquility that has no match. It is where he goes to thank His Rabb for His bounty, to seek His help in difficulty and to gain closeness to Him.

Finally Allahﷻ directed Rasoolullahﷺ to say:

Ana'am 6: 162-63 *"Say: Verily! My worship and my sacrifice and my living and my dying are for Allah, Rabb of the Worlds. He has no partner. This am I commanded, and I am the first of those who submit (to Him)".*

This, in brief is what the prayer is in Islam and what a Muslim feels and does when he is praying. So if you see a Muslim praying know that he is with his Creator, speaking to Him and his Creator is listening.

What is permitted and what is prohibited in foods, business and entertainment?

Permitted & Prohibited: Basic principle

The basic principle of what is permitted and prohibited in Islam is that anything which is intrinsically beneficial is permitted and anything which is intrinsically harmful is prohibited, irrespective of what society may think of it. For example it is known that bank interest is harmful to society and benefits only the money lenders. That is the reason it is prohibited in every religious theology though today bankers rule the world. Islam doesn't recognize fads and fancies of society because Islamic Law (of what is prohibited and permitted) is Divine and the Muslim believes and trusts that what Allahﷻ said is harmful, is actually harmful and so he abstains from it. He is not arrogant enough to usurp the right of Allahﷻ the lawmaker and to start making or changing the Divine law. He realizes and accepts that it is illogical to believe that the creature knows more about what is good or harmful for itself than its own Creator. So he submits to the instructions of the Creator as conveyed by His Messengerﷺ and lives a life that is full of grace and beauty.

In Islam everything is permitted (Halaal) except that which has been specifically prohibited (Haraam). Anything that is prohibited is prohibited in absolute terms, irrespective of quantity. So for example, any quantity of pork and alcohol is prohibited, no matter how small. Also when a thing is prohibited, everything to do with it is prohibited. For example, pork is prohibited and so is rearing pigs, transporting them, processing pork in a factory or working in such a factory, or owning such a factory; storing, selling, buying (even if it is for others), handling, cooking or serving pork are all prohibited.

What is Haraam (prohibited)?

1. Pork and all pork products.
2. The meat of any Halaal animal which was slaughtered without the name of Allahﷻ being mentioned or which was slaughtered in the name of anyone other than Allahﷻ.
3. Blood and its products.
4. Flesh of all animals which are carnivorous.
5. Flesh of all birds of prey.
6. Alcohol in any form.
7. Drugs (addictive substances) of any kind including cigarettes, heroin, marijuana and all such substances.
8. Gambling in all forms, including horse-racing, casinos, slot machines, lottery, casting lots, poker and other card games for money, betting on cricket and other matches and any other form of gambling which may be invented in the future.
9. Any form of entertainment that involves any form of nakedness, shamelessness, music, promiscuity, free mixing of genders, promotion of bad manners or other social evils.
10. Fortune telling or astrology, Feng-shui, Vaastu or any other superstitious luck theory, lucky charms and so on which may be invented in the future.

11. Interest dealings in all forms and business involving anything which is Haraam (interest based banking etc.)

    (This is not an exhaustive list. For details please consult a scholar)

What do we wear?

Basic principle

We are allowed to wear anything as long as it covers the whole body and does not show it (is not transparent) and is not so tight that the shape of the body is visible.

It is obligatory for the men to compulsorily cover their body at least from above the navel to below the knee and for the woman to cover the whole body including the head and hair; except the face and hands. It is obligatory for the woman to cover her hair so that none of it is visible and to cover her ears and throat leaving only her face and hands visible. She may also cover her face and hands with a face mask and gloves if she likes, but this is voluntary and she is not compelled to do so. The woman must also not dress in public in a way which draws attention to herself but must dress in a dignified manner which inspires respect.

Men are not permitted to wear silk or gold in any form.

It is also preferred for the man to cover his entire body with loosely fitting clothing and his head with a cap or turban because this was the way (Sunnah) of Rasoolullahﷺ and is dignified and adds prestige to himself.

Islam prohibits nakedness of any kind for both men and women.

Keeping this rule in mind, both men and women are permitted to wear anything of their choice in any fashion or fabric.

How do we live with others?

Basic Principle

Allahﷻ said about the Muslims:

A'al Imraan 3:110 *You [Muslims] are the best (most beneficial) of people ever raised up for (the benefit of) all mankind; you enjoin Al-Ma'ruf (all that is good) and forbid Al-Munkar (all that is evil), and you believe in Allah.*

So it is enjoined upon the Muslim to strive to be beneficial to all mankind, irrespective of race, ethnicity, color, class, social status, gender, religion or nationality. Justice is primary and supreme in Islam and justice means the absence of all discrimination. In Islam therefore in terms of people and their rights there is no differentiation between Muslim and non-Muslim. They are all entitled to the same privileges and benefits equally before law. In Islam the law is supreme, not the individual. Rasoolullahﷺ who was the lawmaker (on behalf of Allahﷻ) was himself subject to the same law and didn't consider himself or his family to be above the law. This is one of the major differences between Islam's concept of rulership and the concepts of the Divine Right of Kings and similar ideologies. In Islam the ruler is not above the law and can be taken to task for violating the law. There are numerous examples in history of how this was followed with integrity by pious Muslim rulers.

In Islam there are two kinds of duties that a Muslim is obliged to fulfill: Duties towards Allahﷻ (called Huqooq-ullah – Rights of Allahﷻ) and Duties towards the people (Huqooq-ul-ibaad – Rights of the people).

Rasoolullahﷺ said: 'If someone doesn't fulfill the rights of Allahﷻ, he may still be forgiven because Allahﷻ is free from all want and need. But if someone doesn't fulfill the rights of the people he will not be forgiven unless the person forgives him first.' It must be remembered that for this purpose i.e. fulfilling the rights of people, Islam doesn't differentiate between Muslim and non-Muslim. All people have the same rights depending on their roles. For example the rights of parents on a child are the same whether the parents are Muslim or not. The child must respect them, be kind to them, support them and obey them in every respect except when they tell him to do something that Islam prohibits; like worshiping others than Allahﷻ.

Allahﷻ said: **Ma'aida 5:32** *Because of that We ordained for the Children of Israel (and all mankind) that if anyone killed a person, not in retaliation for murder, or (and) for spreading mischief in the land – <u>it would be as if he killed all mankind</u>; and if anyone saved a life, <u>it would be as if he saved the life of all mankind</u>.*

Rasoolullahﷺ said: Whoever has wronged his brother with regards to his honor or anything else should seek pardon now before the time when neither dinar nor dirham will be of any benefit. At that time if he has good deeds an amount equal to the evil will be taken but if he has none, sins from the wronged person will be taken and put on him.

Rasoolullahﷺ said: 'Beware of the curse of the oppressed for surely there is no veil between him and Allahﷻ.' (Related in Sahih Bukhari).

Translation of Sahih Muslim, Book 32:

The Book of Virtue, Good Manners and Joining of the Ties of Relationship (Kitab Al-Birr was-Salat-I-wa'l-Adab) Book 032, Number 6251:

Abu Hurairah☆ reported Rasoolullah☆ as saying: *Do you know who is destitute? They (the Companions) said: The destitute amongst us is the one who has neither dirham nor dinar (money and material wealth). He (Rasoolullah☆) said: The poor of my Ummah is the one who will come on the Day of Resurrection with prayers and fasts and Zakat but (he will find himself bankrupt on that day as he would have exhausted his funds of virtues) since he hurled abuses upon others, brought calumny against others and unlawfully consumed the wealth of others and shed the blood of others and beat others. His virtues will be credited to the account of the one (who suffered at his hands). And if his good deeds fall short to clear the account, then the sins of the victim will be entered in (his account) and he will be thrown in the Hell-Fire.*

Narrated Abdullah ibn Mas'ud☆: A man asked Rasoolullah☆, "How can I know when I do well and when I do ill?" He replied, *"When you hear your neighbors say you have done well, you have done well and when you hear them say you have done ill, you have done ill."* (Related by Al-Tirmidhi)

Narrated Abdullah ibn Umar☆: Rasoolullah☆ said, *"The best friend in the sight of Allah☆ is the well-wisher of his companions and the best neighbor is one who behaves the best towards his neighbors."* (Related by Al-Tirmidhi)

About justice Allahﷻ said:

An-Nisa 4:135 O you who believe! Stand out firmly for justice as witnesses to Allah even as against yourselves or your parents or your kin and whether it be (against) rich or poor: for Allah can best protect both. Follow not the lusts (of your hearts) lest you swerve (from justice) and if you distort (justice) or decline to do justice verily Allah is well-acquainted with all that you do.

Once again no differentiation between Muslim and non-Muslim. Justice after all means not to discriminate. Islam doesn't. There are numerous incidents where judges in the Islamic Khilaafa Raashida (The Islamic Rightly Guided Caliphate – refers to the rule of the first 5 Khulafa – Caliphs) and during the rule of other pious Muslim rulers, ruled in favor of non-Muslims and against Muslims.

Rasoolullahﷺ said, *"The world is like a ship and mankind are its passengers. The welfare of all depends on the safe conduct of each. If anyone is found making a hole in the side of the ship, he must be stopped."*

Rasoolullahﷺ said, *"The pinnacle of faith is to speak for justice in the face of a tyrant."*

This focus on justice doesn't imply the absence of compassion. Compassion is encouraged as is forgiveness. To the extent that even in the case of murder, the family of the victim are given the choice either to accept money and spare the life of the killer or even to forgive him altogether. Based on the circumstances, the court can admit either of these options. So also in the case of a loan being given to a person;

Islam clearly directs the lender to be compassionate with the borrower and not only, not charge interest (which is clearly Haraam) but also not to insist on repayment until the person is able to do it without hardship. And to top it all, the lender is told that if he foregoes the repayment altogether, then that is better for him in the sight of Allahﷻ.

Rasoolullahﷺ is reported to have said that it is more virtuous to give a person an interest free loan than to give him that amount as charity. When he was asked why it was more virtuous to give a loan which you would expect to be returned compared to charity which is a gift, he replied, 'Because you give the loan when he needs it and the charity when you feel like giving it.' Justice and compassion are inextricably linked. It is compassion to ensure that the victim of a crime gets justice. Islam therefore places more importance on the rights of the victim than on so-called human rights of the criminal who unilaterally decided to violate the human rights of the victim in the first place. Modern society seems to have lost its balance in this among many other matters and so its punishments don't deter criminals from continuing their activities.

Ask anyone who has been the victim of violent crime what he or she thinks about the idea of exemplary punishments which discourage potential aspirants and you will find that they will all agree with the Divine Islamic punishments which may seem harsh only when looked at in isolation without any reference to the holistic law of cause and effect.

In the light of all these teachings and Ayaat of the Qur'an it is clear that Islam places a very high premium on justice because it is only when justice is established that one can have peace, harmony and safety for everyone. That is the reason why for centuries Jews, Christians and Hindus lived in peace and harmony and great prosperity under Muslim rule. Many of them rose to great heights in government, business and academics while still remaining in their own religions. In the rule of the Khilaafa Raashida and the rule of pious Muslim rulers anywhere in the world, there was no persecution of non-Muslims on account of their religion. History is witness to this. Muslim rulers who persecuted anyone on account of their religion were acting against the tenets of Islam. Islam is not answerable for their conduct. They are answerable to Allahﷻ for violating Islamic law and will pay the price.

There was and is no compulsion on anyone to enter Islam. If anyone enters Islam, he does so because he is convinced that Islam is the truth and he wants to believe in it and to live by its laws.

The most impressive example of treating even enemies well comes, not surprisingly, from the life of Rasoolullahﷺ himself. At the time that Makkah was conquered the conduct of Rasoolullahﷺ's soldiers became a source of inspiration for those who they vanquished. People who were vanquished saw the way Rasoolullahﷺ entered Makkah, not arrogantly as a victor but with his head lowered in submission to His Rabb.

Thanking Him for the victory, granting amnesty and protection to his erstwhile enemies who had persecuted him so mercilessly and not exacting revenge which is what they expected him to do. This is the finest example of how Muslims live with others and the reason why Islam spread all over the world so quickly– because Islam and Muslims won the hearts of others. This was the secret of the Companions of Rasoolullahﷺ and it must become our way today.

Interestingly in modern times, this example of Rasoolullahﷺ was repeated by President Nelson Mandela when South Africa became free from Apartheid rule and the new government adopted the principle of reconciliation and forgiveness instead of revenge and retribution, with respect to those who had oppressed them and violated their rights. The results are visible for all to see. South Africa continues to be the most stable of African countries and the most sought after place of residence notwithstanding various other issues. It is not my purpose to delve in detail about South African politics here. I mentioned only the very usual and remarkable step that President Nelson Mandela took when he took charge as the first post-apartheid President.

How do we deal with money?

Islam places great importance on financial matters. The principal that is followed is that all financial dealings must result in the greater good of society with special reference to the poor.

Not only does Islam strongly encourage charity but it actually makes charity obligatory to the extent that it is directly linked, conditionally, with faith itself. This obligatory charity is called Zakat and generally is 2.5% of accumulated wealth that has been in the possession of the owner for 12 months. Zakat is compulsory on anyone who has the minimum specified amount of wealth (please see below). Zakat is wealth tax and not income tax. It is liable on wealth that is not in circulation and one of its purposes is to keep money in circulation and to discourage hoarding.

It is not my purpose to state all the rules relating to Zakat and so if you have any specific questions please refer to a scholar who is learned in Zakat matters. I am stating here the general principles relating to Zakat to give you a feel for this unique principle of Islam and how important it is to create a healthy society. A society that is ridden with huge economic disparities is sick. Zakat is the cure. Modern societies would do well to learn from Islam.

Nisaab ul-Zakat (qualifying amount for Zakat) for N*aqd* (gold and silver) is defined as the minimum amount of *Naqd* specified by *Shari'ah* below which one is not required to pay Zakat, whereas if one's wealth is equal to or exceeds it then Zakat becomes obligatory.

Zakat ul-maal (wealth) in *Shari'ah* is required for the two types of *Naqd*—gold and silver—and what serves their function in modern times (currency or cash), whether it is dollars or riyals or pounds or any other currency.

Nisaab for gold as Rasoolullahﷺ informed us (and for currencies made from gold) is 20 *Mithqaalan,* a measure which is equivalent to 85 grams of pure gold (1 *Mithqaal* = 4.25 grams). It becomes obligatory upon anyone who owns such an amount in any form to pay Zakat on it to the extent of 2.5% of its value and give that to the poor.

Nisaab for silver and currencies made from silver is 200 *dirhams,* which is equivalent to 595 grams of pure silver (1 *dirham* = 2.975 grams). Likewise, it becomes obligatory upon anyone who owns such an amount in any form to pay Zakat on it to the extent of 2.5% of its value and give that to the poor.

It is well known that there is a noticeable disparity between the value of *Nisaab* for gold and that of silver in our times. The best and most conservative way to calculate Zakat is to assess how much money has been in our possession for a complete lunar year (Hijri, which is 354 days). The easiest way is to calculate Zakat on a specific day each year on whatever cash, gold or silver may be in our possession on that day. If the amount reaches the value of *Nisaab* for silver or more, then he should pay from it for every 1000 dollars, 25 dollars (i.e. 2.5%) to be given to those prescribed as beneficiaries as specified by Shari'ah.

The most important thing to remember is that if someone refuses to accept that Zakat is obligatory then he has left Islam.

In addition to Zakat there is a huge emphasis on voluntary charity in Islam. Muslims collectively are arguably the most generous and charitable people in the world. There are many Ayaat in the Qur'an where Allahﷻ encourages charity and promises great reward. Allahﷻ said:

Al-Baqara 2:254 O You who believe! Spend of that with which We have provided for you before a Day comes when there will be no bargaining, nor friendship not intercession. And it is the disbelievers who are the Zalimun (wrong doers)

Al-Baqara 2:261 The likeness of those who spend their wealth in the Way of Allah is the likeness of a grain (of corn). It grows seven ears, and each ears has hundred grains. Allah gives manifold increase to whom He wills. And is All-Sufficient for His creatures needs, All-Knower. **262** *Those who spend their wealth in the Cause of Allah and do not follow up their gifts with reminders of their generosity or with injury, their reward is with their Lord. On them shall be no fear nor shall they grieve.*

This is also the reason why dealing in interest is so strongly prohibited in Islam. Interest destroys wealth and oppresses the weak. The lender is not interested in the welfare of the one who he lends to and is interested only in the return on his capital. Borrowers are encouraged to live outside their means and not to save and live within their means. All these are things that create social hardship and increase the gap between rich and poor. Islam therefore strongly prohibits dealing in interest. Allahﷻ declared war on those who deal in interest.

Al-Baqara 2:275 *Those who gorge themselves on usury (all interest based dealings) behave but as he might behave whom Satan has confounded with his touch; for they say, "Buying and selling is but a kind of usury" - the while Allah has made buying and selling lawful and usury unlawful. Hence, whoever becomes aware of his Sustainer's admonition, and thereupon desists [from usury - (all interest based dealings) may keep his past gains, and it will be for Allah to judge him; but as for those who return to it -they are destined for the fire, therein to abide!* **2:276** *Allah deprives usurious gains (all gains from interest based dealings)of all blessing, whereas He blesses charitable deeds with manifold increase. And Allah does not love anyone who is stubbornly ungrateful and persists in sinful ways.*

2:278 *O you who have attained to faith! Fear Allah. and give up all outstanding gains from usury (all interest based dealings) if you are [truly] believers;*

2:279 *For if you don't do it, then know that you are at war with Allah and His Messenger. But if you repent, then you shall be entitled to [the return of] your principal: you will do no wrong, and neither will you be wronged.*

Islam permits all forms of trade and business provided the material being traded or the business being conducted is in permitted things. For example it is not permitted to deal in anything which is Haraam, e.g. pig products, alcohol, cigarettes, gambling of any kind, interest based banking and so on.

The basic principle as mentioned earlier is that if something is prohibited then all forms of dealing in it are also prohibited and so businesses which deal in those would also be prohibited. Other than that Muslims are permitted to do business or work in any area that they may choose.

The purpose of the Islamic economic system is not to support greed – the basis of the capitalist system – but to encourage effort and industry and to promote equity and compassion and to reduce economic disparities. Islam not only encouraged but made social responsibility obligatory on the rich centuries before the world invented the term CSR (Corporate Social Responsibility). In the Islamic system it is not only corporations who need to be socially responsible but every single individual.

Imagine a society where the rich search for the poor to help because they have to discharge a responsibility that they will be questioned about. Imagine a society where the lender lends money with the intention to help, not with the intention to make more money. Imagine a society which encourages entrepreneurship through venture capital financing and meaningful participation of the owner of the capital and the owner of the idea both working together to build a successful enterprise. Imagine a society where the rich implement welfare projects as a means of their own salvation in the Hereafter.

Self interest in Islam is linked inextricably with public interest and social welfare. People are encouraged to save, live frugal lives, be conscious of their obligation to those who have less than them and seek only to please Allahﷻ. As mentioned earlier, Islam doesn't differentiate between Muslim and non-Muslim as regards the beneficiaries of charity. So everyone benefits irrespective of religious affiliation. This is the essence of Applied Islam.

History is witness to societies ruled by Muslims which practiced these principles for centuries and lived in great harmony and plenty. History is also witness to their degeneration when a few, overcome with greed, broke the rules and created suffering and bad blood. In my view, the principle is proved even if it succeeds once. That has happened many times over. All that remains now is for us to once again change our ways and go back to our basic principles commanded by Allahﷻ through His Messengerﷺ.

The world is reeling under centuries of economic oppression. It is desperately seeking a solution. Islam has the solution. All that is needed is for Muslims to wake up to this fact and take the solution to the world and to demonstrate its effectiveness by practicing it themselves and showing working models of excellence for the world to emulate. Islam gave thought leadership to the world. Muslims need to accept this responsibility once again and stop chasing the material world like everyone else.

Common questions asked about Islam

First, a disclaimer

It is not possible or feasible for me to imagine all questions that may possibly exist. So I have tried to answer the most common ones.

The idea of this section, as well as of this whole book is to provide in a dispassionate and logical manner, accurate information about Islam so that stereotypes are dispelled. Stereotypes are the result of ignorance and understanding comes from knowing facts.

Do feel free to write to me or even better to speak to your Muslim neighbors, friends and acquaintances, visit the nearest mosque or Islamic Center where you live and ask frank questions. Naturally you will ask them in a polite and respectful manner, I am sure, because that is the best way to understand others.

Ask politely, listen carefully, thank them for sharing information and make up your own mind.

Questions

1. Is it true that Islam means 'Peace'?
2. What does Islam say about other Prophets?
3. What does the Qur'an say about Jesus?
4. What is Jihad?
5. Hijab: Oppression or Liberation?
6. What are the rights of women in Islam?
7. What is Islamic Fundamentalism – Is it fact or fiction?
8. What is Sufism and what is its connection with Islam?

Is it true that Islam means 'Peace'?

Question: How can we say that Islam is a religion of peace when it advocates all kinds of violence and its believers engage in violence in many places in the world?

Answer: This type of question is very common in the present day and very easy to answer provided the questioner is willing to do three things:

1. Some research into Islam on his own
2. Willingness to separate facts from propaganda
3. Willingness to separate what Islam advocates as a religion from what people professing to be Muslims may do at any given point in time.

Before we look at each in some detail, my advice to those people who selectively quote from the Qur'an in an effort to 'prove' that Islam advocates violence; we need to remember some facts about the revelation of the Qur'an.

The Qur'an was revealed over a period of 23 years and has several different kinds of ayahs (verses):

1. Ayaat (verses) relating to the doctrine of belief in One God, types of worship (Salah, fasting, zakat, hajj and so on), relationship with God, fear and love of God and so on.
2. Ayaat relating to social and political issues and orders regarding them (charity, inheritance, people's rights and duties, virtue, manners, gender relations, marriage, obedience to Rasoolullah ﷺ and so on).

3. Ayaat relating to the history of past people and their Prophets (Moses, Jesus, Noah etc.) as a way of learning lessons from their lives and times.
4. Ayaat relating to things of the unknown (some of which have become known now due to scientific development and confirm what the Qur'an said 14 centuries ago): how the universe was created, development of the human fetus, roots of mountains, movement of tectonic plates, separation of oceans, life after death, Day of Judgment, Heaven (Jannah) and Hell (Jahannam), nature of the soul and so on.
5. Ayaat that were revealed at the time of particular incidents such as battle orders, instructions to deal with some peculiar situation of the time, interpretation of happenings or glad tidings as a result of the actions of Rasoolullahﷺ and His Companions or answers to the questions that people used to ask Rasoolullahﷺ for which Allahﷻ would send him the answers.

It is a critical part of the study of the Qur'an to study the circumstances of the particular revelation (asbaab-un-nuzool) without which it is entirely possible to misunderstand the meaning of the ayah as one does not understand it contextually. This is particularly true of the ayahs revealed at the time of particular happenings or events which applied only to that time and those people and are not universal in application in the normal sense. What remains however is, that if such situations happen again then the orders in those Ayaat would be applicable in such a case.

A good case in point is the orders concerning the treatment of slaves (prisoners of war who used to become slaves). In today's world these instructions are not applicable since we don't have slaves and prisoners of war are lodged in prisons and are not given to individuals to keep as servants. However if ever a situation emerged where a Muslim had control of another person in the role of a slave, the Qur'an advocates that he should either free him or treat him well and look after his welfare if he retained him in that role. More about this in relation to the Ayaat about warfare later in this chapter.

Without the knowledge of the context of revelation it is therefore clear that one cannot understand the meaning or scope of application of the ayah.

This is a basic, foundational (primary school level) rule when studying the Qur'an. Very basic and foundational and so very important. To illustrate with an example of the scope for misunderstanding when the context is ignored let me take an example from another source, the Bhagavad Gita. If one were to read the conversation of Krishna with Arjuna in the Bhagavad Gita without understanding the context of the whole story of Mahabharata, it is entirely possible to come to the conclusion that the Gita advocates the killing of one brother by another, killing of the father by the sons, the destruction of family, and even the attacking of teachers by their students in order to gain land and kingdom.

But if one reads the whole Mahabharata and then interprets the above verses, it is perfectly clear that Krishna's comments related to the dilemma of Arjuna and to his moral crisis when he faced the army of the 'enemy' which actually comprised of his own family; his grandfather, cousins, nephews and even his teacher Dronacharya. In the context, they make sense.

To give another example if one were to read the battle orders of the US Army in Vietnam and come to the conclusion that it is the duty of every American citizen to kill every Vietnamese citizen wherever he finds him, then one could rightfully be accused of stupidity of a marked degree or of deliberately distorting facts and quoting them out of context to cause mischief.

This is the most common mistake that all criticizers of Islam and Muslims make when in their hurry and desperation to find something negative they try to 'cherry-pick' and quote Ayaat from the Qur'an with either no knowledge of the context of the revelation or by deliberately hiding it hoping that their readers are too stupid or lazy to do their own research to find the truth. But even a rudimentary level of research will show-up the falsehood they speak.

What makes absolute sense and is most reasonable when studied in context appears unreasonable when seen out of context. Another very major mistake that such people make, which leads one to suspect their very intention, is that they conveniently ignore all the Ayaat (verses) that say the opposite. This shows up clearly the attempt at trying to distort the message of the Qur'an.

Any serious researcher can quickly see through this lame strategy and come to the correct conclusion about the mischief that they intend.

Finally it is important to remember that in any pluralistic society, there will be many faiths and belief systems, each naturally professing to be the best one. This is perfectly natural in that if this were not the case then that system would not have any uniqueness about it. For example the Communists believe their system is the best and the Capitalists believe the opposite. Even within the same faith, be it Christianity or Hinduism different sects have different beliefs and formulae for success in this life and the Hereafter. Coke may accept that the world has the freedom to drink Pepsi but it will never say that Pepsi is as good as Coke or that it doesn't matter what you drink. Such is life.

In any free society we have no quarrel with the beliefs of anyone, even if according to that particular belief, we are considered unsuccessful in the Hereafter. People of all faiths are welcome to live with their beliefs and it is this freedom that we cherish in a free society. We don't demand that they change their belief or their theology as it relates to metaphysical matters. It is acceptable in a free society to hold different beliefs and to disagree without rancor and bad blood on that account. Strange how this is forgotten by some people nowadays in their anxiety to criticize others without even taking the trouble to see if there is anything to be critical about.

However what is a matter of concern is how people of any faith are ordered to act, (especially with respect to those who don't share their belief) in this life and world. In the context of Islam, to understand this it is necessary to see orders and instructions in the Qur'an that are not specific to a particular situation and the people who were facing it at the time of Rasoolullahﷺ but at those orders that are for all Muslims, for all time. This list is too long and exhaustive to include here but I have included a couple of things to show that there is nothing in Islam, the Qur'an, the Shari'ah or the Hadith to advocate violence, killing of innocent people, ill treatment of anyone irrespective of their religion or the spread of terror in the land.

On the contrary, there is the most severe castigation and the promise of punishment in the Hereafter for anyone who does such things even if he is a Muslim.

For those who want to study and find out and are genuinely curious, there is plenty of proof. For those who want to spread mischief however, proof is the last thing they want. Such people will always be there and will always fail as they have always failed. For the truth always prevails over falsehood. This is the promise of the Qur'an and its writer, Allahﷻ the One and Only Creator of all that exists and the One and Only worthy of worship.

To look at the three things that I have advocated:

1. Some research into Islam on their own
2. Willingness to separate facts from propaganda
3. Willingness to separate what Islam advocates as a religion from what people professing to be Muslims may do at any given point in time.

Some research into Islam on their own

The first thing to understand is that Islam is a religion based on a Book (Qur'an) and the interpretation of that book by its Prophet. So everything is documented and available for scrutiny. The book is the Qur'an and the interpretation is the Hadith or Sunnah. These are the only two sources of theological doctrine in Islam. Anyone who takes the trouble to read these in any detail will see the clear emphasis on a constructive developmental perspective for the world. Everything in Islam is based on the good it does for society and people. There is nothing at all which is destructive.

Even punishments are prescribed in relation to the harm to society that the crime causes. So punishments for crimes which are likely to cause disruption of society or a breakdown in its moral values have the most serious punishments prescribed for them.

I will suffice to quote only one or two Ayaat of the Qur'an in this context and leave the rest to the questioner himself to discover. That way he will believe his own eyes rather more than believing me.

Al Ma'aidah 5:32 Because of that We ordained for the Children of Israel (and all mankind) that if anyone killed a person, not in retaliation of murder, or (and) for spreading mischief in the land – <u>it would be as if he killed all mankind</u>; and if anyone saved a life, <u>it would be as if he saved the life of all mankind</u>. And indeed there came to them (all mankind) Our Messengers with clear proofs, evidences and signs; even then after that many of them continued to exceed the limits (committing major sins, oppressing) in the land.

Kahf 18:29 And say: "The truth is from your Lord." Then whosoever wills let him believe: and whosoever wills, let him disbelieve.

Baqara 2: 256 There is no compulsion in religion. Verily the Right Path has become distinct from the wrong path. And whoever disbelieves in the Taghut (false things) and believes in Allah then he has grasped the most trustworthy handhold that will never break. And Allâh is the All-Hearer, All-Knower.

Kafiroon 109 Say (O Mohammad) O You who deny the truth, I worship not that which you worship. Nor will you worship that which I worship. And I shall not worship that which you worship. Nor will you worship that which I worship. To you be your religion and to me my religion.

Hadith: Narrated Abdullah ibn Mas'ud: A man said to the Prophet, "How can I know when I do well and when I do ill?" He replied, *"When you hear your neighbors say you have done well, you have done well and when you hear them say you have done ill, you have done ill."* Al-Tirmidhi

Hadith: Narrated Abdullah ibn Umar: The Prophet said, *"The best friend in the sight of Allah is the well-wisher of his*

companions and the best neighbor is one who behaves the best towards his neighbors." Al Tirmidhi

Hadith: Narrated Anas bin Malik: The Prophet said, "The biggest of Al Kaba'air (the great sins) are:

1. *To join others as partners in worship with Allah*

2. *To murder a human being.*

3. *To be undutiful to one's parents.*

4. *To make a false statement or 'to give false witness'.*

(Related in Sahih Bukhari, Vol. 9, Hadith 10.)

As I said, for a Muslim and for anyone who is a serious enquirer or scholar of Islam, these Ayaat and these Ahadith and their import are clear enough. These are the orders of Allah and Rasoolullah and in Islamic theological doctrine anyone who deliberately disobeys an order of Allah or Rasoolullah places himself outside the fold of Islam.

There is not a single instance in the Qur'an or the Sunnah where Islam has advocated, permitted or even remotely suggested the killing of innocent people or terrorist activity in any form whatsoever. This is a challenge to anyone to try to find any verse of the Qur'an or an authentic teaching of Rasoolullah which advocates killing innocent people irrespective of their religion.

Islamic Law (the much maligned Shari'ah) prescribes total equality between people in all respects on points of law with Muslims getting no preference at all. The rights of neighbors for example are irrespective of the religion of the neighbor. However some people choose to believe false propaganda rather than investigating the truth. Islam is a religion that came for all mankind and so its laws relate to all mankind.

It does not advocate anything that is good for some and bad for others. And it punishes anyone seeking to harm innocent people.

Willingness to separate facts from propaganda

To quote an eminent (Christian) writer on this subject, John Esposito, who is an advisor to the US Government on Islamic affairs, in his book, 'The Islamic Threat': *"Much of the reassertion of religion in politics and society has been subsumed under the term 'Islamic fundamentalism'. Although 'fundamentalism' is a common designation, in the press and increasingly among academics it is used in a variety of ways. For a number of reasons, it tells us everything and yet nothing. First, all those who call for a return to foundational beliefs or the 'fundamentals' of a religion may be called fundamentalist.*

In a strict sense this could include all practicing Muslims, who accept the Qur'an as the literal word of God and the Sunnah (example) of the Prophet Muhammad as a normative model for living. Second, our understanding and perceptions of fundamentalism are heavily influenced by American Protestantism. Webster's Ninth New Collegiate Dictionary defines the term fundamentalism - as a "movement in the 20th century Protestantism emphasizing the literally interpreted Bible as fundamental to Christian life and teaching." For many liberal or mainline Christians, "fundamentalist" is pejorative and derogatory, being applied rather indiscriminately to all those who advocate a literalist biblical position and thus are regarded as static, retrogressive and extremist. As a result, fundamentalism often has been regarded popularly as referring to those who are literalists and wish to return to and replicate the past. In fact, few individuals or organizations in the Middle East fit such a stereotype. Indeed, many fundamentalist leaders have had the best education, enjoy responsible positions in society and create viable modern institutions such as schools, hospitals, and social service agencies".

Mohammed, The Prophet

By Prof. K. S. Ramakrishna Rao, Head of the Department of Philosophy, Government College for Women University of Mysore, Mandya-571401 (Karnataka). **Re-printed from "Islam and Modern age", Hyderabad, March 1978.**

"The theory of Islam and Sword for instance is not heard now frequently in any quarter worth the name. **The principle of Islam that there is no compulsion in religion is well known.**

Gibbon, a historian of world repute says, *"A pernicious tenet has been imputed to Mohammadans, the duty of extirpating all the religions by sword. This charge based on ignorance and bigotry, is refuted by Qur'an, by history of Musalman conquerors and by their public and legal toleration of Christian worship. The great success of Mohammad's life had been effected by sheer moral force, without a stroke of sword."*

Mahatma Gandhi: *"Someone has said that Europeans in South Africa dread the advent of Islam -- Islam that civilized Spain, Islam that took the torch light to Morocco and preached to the world the gospel of brotherhood. The Europeans of South Africa dread the Advent of Islam. They may claim equality with the white races.* ***They may well dread it, if brotherhood is a sin. If it is equality of colored races then their dread is well founded.****"*

Today we live in a world that is so colored by anti-Muslim propaganda that anyone who is willing to criticize Muslims and Islam (especially if that person is himself a Muslim) is given a public platform and is published. In all such cases neither the writer, publisher nor even the readers care if the writing is factual or simply hate literature masquerading as fiction, humor or something else. Salman Rushdie, Tasleema Nasreen and so on are famous in this respect. But it is interesting to see what non-Muslim writers, who are recognized as serious scholars and teachers have to say on the same subject. We have a choice about who we want to believe.

If one only reads a history of Palestine and the record of Israel and its apartheid oppression, one can't fail to commend the resilience and courage of the people of that wretched land.

The solution to the Palestinian problem is amazingly simple: Get Israel to return the land to its rightful owners and stop terrorizing them. Give them a true voice in the councils of the world and get the powers of the world to recognize the atrocities that the regime in Israel has been perpetrating on the helpless people of Palestine and stop supporting them and force them to pay compensation. How one would price a murdered child is a debatable point but that can be debated when we are ready to think. But for some of us it is easier to blame the helpless ones.

There are many such examples of oppression of Muslims without any cause other than that they believe in Allahﷻ and then crying foul when they fight back with whatever means they have. Chechnya, Afghanistan, Iraq, Bosnia, Kosovo, Gujarat……..the list is endless and it is added to every day.

It is good to remember that peace is very desirable and worth working for. But peace is an effect and not a cause. Peace is the effect of the establishment of justice. That is the cause which results in peace. But to make that happen it means having the courage to accept facts and to condemn oppression. Until the world is unwilling to do that and supports oppression when it is done by the powerful, true peace will only be a mirage on the horizon and any truce, a recess between wars.

Willingness to separate what Islam advocates as a religion from what people professing to be Muslims may do at any given point in time

This should be easy for people who are used to doing this for everyone else. But somehow for some of us applying double standards is easier.

1. Haven't we seen Sinn Fein and IRA violence for decades? Where have we called it Roman Catholic or Christian terrorism?
2. Haven't we seen Israeli terrorism for the last 54 years? Where have we called it Jewish or Zionist terrorism?
3. Haven't we seen South African, apartheid with countless atrocities visited on the heads of the black African freedom fighters (Nelson Mandela being their leader) called terrorists by the White South African regime. Where have we seen it called Christian Calvinist Protestant terrorism?
4. Haven't we seen the oppression of the Dalits in India by the Upper Castes for centuries? Where have we called it Hindu or Brahmin terrorism?
5. Haven't we seen the slaughter of innocent Muslims in Gujarat (the latest of many such pogroms since 1947)? Where have we called it Gujarati or Hindu terrorism?
6. Haven't we seen the slaughter of Muslims by Greek Orthodox Christians in Bosnia and Kosovo? Where have we called it Serbian, Christian terrorism?
7. Haven't we seen Muslims slaughtered by Russians and Americans in Afghanistan, Chechnya, Iraq? Where have we called it American or Russian terrorism?

So when we see a Muslim fighting in desperation after having seen his home and family destroyed by an enemy that is brutal, powerful and totally pitiless, why do we call it Islamic terrorism?

As I said, if we want facts, and want to be fair; that is a choice we have. If on the other hand we want to believe propaganda, close our eyes to reality and ascribe blame falsely, that too is our choice. And like all choices, each one has a price. We are free to choose and pay the price.

What does Islam say about other Prophets?

Before we look at what Islam says about other prophets it will be instructive to read for example, traditional Christian doctrine about Islam and its prophet Muhammadﷺ. The language of hatred, calumny, deliberate distortion and prejudice will leave you breathless. No wonder there is so much hatred for Islam; not because of anything Muslims do or did but purely due to the brainwashing of simple, ordinary Christians all over Europe by the Church - in whichever denomination.

Interestingly in my view this is the main reason why so many Christians are turning to Islam because when they see the facts they are so positively-shocked and so pleasantly surprised that they spontaneously accept the truth which they are faced with. The hate propaganda of the Church and its allies is actually opening the eyes of Christians. Truly Allahﷻ guides who He wills to the truth.

Islam's view about prophets is as follows: Allahﷻ said that Messengers were sent to all people everywhere from time to time. Then as the message of the Messenger was altered and changed other Messengers were sent to remind the people of their duty to their Lord. All Messengers came with the same message: That there's nobody worthy of worship except Allahﷻ. A message of unity of worship, a message prohibiting polytheism, promoting good, ethical and moral behavior and prohibiting evil, unethical and immoral behavior.

Allahﷻ says: ***Ar-Ra'ad 13:7*** *And the disbelievers say: "Why is not a sign sent down to him from his Lord?" You are only a Warner, and to every people there is a guide.*

Muslims believe specifically in all the Messengers of Allahﷻ whose names He revealed in the Qur'an or who we were informed about by Rasoolullahﷺ. Allahﷻ says:

Baqara 2: 285 *The Messenger (Muhammad) believes in what has been sent down to him from his Lord, and (so do) the believers. Each one believes in Allâh, His Angels, His Books, and His Messengers. They say, "We make no distinction between one or another of His Messengers" - and they say, "We hear, and we obey. (We seek) Your Forgiveness, our Lord, and to You is the return (of all)."*

The Messengers mentioned in the Qur'an and Sunnah include Adam, Idris, Sheeth, Nuh, Hud, Saleh, Ibrahim, Ismail, Lut, Shuaib, Ishaaq, Yaqoob, Yusuf, Ayub, Yunus, Musa, Yusha, Dawud, Sulaiman, Zakaria, Yahya, Isa, Mohammad (Allahﷻ's mercy and blessings on them all). In addition to these, it is the belief of Muslims that Messengers were sent to all people of all time though all are not mentioned. Rasoolullahﷺ mentioned that more than 124,000 Messengers were sent to mankind. Allahﷻ knows best the exact number of His Messengers.

Allahﷻ said that some of these Messengers have a higher status than others but to give this status is a prerogative of Allahﷻ and not for human beings to be concerned with.

***Baqara* 2:253**   *Those Messengers! We preferred some to others; to some of them Allâh spoke (directly); others He raised to degrees (of honor); and to 'Iesa (Jesus), the son of Maryam (Mary), We gave clear proofs and evidences, and supported him with Rûh-ul-Qudus [Jibreel].*

***Al-Ahqaf* 46:35** *Therefore be patient (O Muhammad) as did the Messengers of strong will and be in no haste about them (disbelievers).*

The number of Ulul-Azm Minar Rusul (The Messengers of Strong Will – an address of special honor) are 5: Nuh, Ibrahim, Musa, Eesa and Muhammad (Peace and blessings be on them all).

It is the Muslim doctrine that we believe that Allahﷻ sent Messengers to all people but we also believe specifically in the ones that He named. As for people known as leaders of others like Buddha and so on, we don't believe that they were the Messengers of Allahﷻ because Allahﷻ did not name them. Our position about them is that we are not aware of their status with Allahﷻ.

What does the Qur'an say about Jesus?

Jesus has a very special place in Islam, of high honor along with Moses and the father of the prophets, Ibrahim (Peace be on them all). About Jesus, Allahﷻ says:

An-Nisa 4:171 *O people of the Scripture (Jews and Christians)! Do not exceed the limits in your religion, nor say of Allâh aught but the truth. The Messiah 'Iesa (Jesus), son of Maryam (Mary), was (no more than) a Messenger of Allâh and His Word, ("Be!"- and he was) which He bestowed on Maryam (Mary) and a spirit (Rûh) created by Him; so believe in Allâh and His Messengers. Say not: "Three (trinity)!" Cease! (it is) better for you. For Allâh is (the only) One Ilâh (God), Glory be to Him (Far Exalted is He) above having a son. To Him belongs all that is in the heavens and all that is in the earth. And Allâh is All Sufficient as a Disposer of affairs. The Messiah would never be arrogant enough to reject to be a slave of Allâh, nor the angels who are near (to Allâh). And whosoever rejects His worship and is proud, then He will gather them all together unto Himself. So, as for those who believed (in the Oneness of Allâh - Islâmic Monotheism) and did deeds of righteousness, He will give their (due) rewards, and more out of His Bounty. But as for those who refuse His worship and were arrogant, He will punish them with a painful torment. And they will not find for themselves besides Allâh any protector or helper.*

Maaidah 5:109. *On the Day when Allâh will gather the Messengers together and say to them: "What was the response you received (from men to your teaching)? They will say: "We have no knowledge, verily, only You are the All Knower of all that is hidden (or unseen, etc.)."* **110.** *(Remember) when Allâh will say (on the Day of Resurrection). "O 'Iesa (Jesus), son of Maryam (Mary)! Remember My Favour to you and to your mother when I supported you with Rûh ul Qudus [Jibrael (Gabriel)] so that you spoke to the people in the cradle and in maturity; and when I taught you writing, Al Hikmah (the power of understanding), the Taurât (Torah) and the Injeel (Gospel); and when you made out of the clay, as it were, the figure of a bird, by My Permission, and you breathed into it, and it became a bird by My Permission, and you healed those born blind, and the lepers by My Permission, and when you brought forth the dead by My Permission; and when I restrained the Children of Israel from you (when they resolved to kill you) since you came unto them with clear proofs, and the disbelievers among them said: 'This is nothing but evident magic.'* **111.** *And when I (Allâh) put in the hearts of Al-Hawârîeen (the Disciples) [of 'Iesa (Jesus)] to believe in Me and My Messenger, they said: "We believe. And bear witness that we are Muslims."* **112.** *(Remember) when Al-Hawârîûn (the disciples) said: "O 'Iesa (Jesus), son of Maryam (Mary)! Can your Lord send down to us a table spread (with food) from heaven?" 'Iesa (Jesus) said: "Fear Allâh, if you are indeed believers."* **113.** *They said: "We wish to eat thereof and to be stronger in Faith, and to know that you have indeed told us the truth and that we ourselves be its witnesses."* **114.** *'Iesa (Jesus), son of Maryam (Mary), said: "O Allâh, our Lord! Send us from heaven a table spread (with food) that there may be for us - for the first and the last of us - a festival and a sign from You; and provide us sustenance, for You are the Best of sustainers."* **115.** *Allâh said: "I am going to send it down unto you, but if any of you after that disbelieves, then I will punish him with a torment such as I have not inflicted on anyone among*

*(all) the 'Alamîn (mankind and jinns)."***116.** *And (remember) when Allâh will say (on the Day of Resurrection): "O 'Iesa (Jesus), son of Maryam (Mary)! Did you say unto men: 'Worship me and my mother as two gods besides Allâh?' " He will say: "Glory be to You! It was not for me to say what I had no right (to say). Had I said such a thing, You would surely have known it. You know what is in my inner self though I do not know what is in Yours, truly, You, only You, are the All Knower of all that is hidden and unseen.***117.** *"Never did I say to them anything except what You (Allâh) did command me to say: 'Worship Allâh, my Lord and your Lord.' And I was a witness over them while I dwelt amongst them, but when You took me up, You were the Watcher over them, and You are a Witness to all things. (Christians of the world to note how their religion has been changed).***118.** *"If You punish them, they are Your slaves, and if You forgive them, verily You, only You are the All Mighty, the All Wise."***119.** *Allâh will say: "This is a Day on which the truthful will profit from their truth: theirs are Gardens under which rivers flow (in Paradise) - they shall abide therein forever. Allâh is pleased with them and they with Him. That is the great success (Paradise).***120.** *To Allâh belongs the dominion of the heavens and the earth and all that is therein, and He is Able to do all things.*

Ma'aidah 5: 15 *O people of the Scripture (Jews and Christians)! Now has come to you Our Messenger (Muhammad) explaining to you much of that which you used to hide from the Scripture and pass over (i.e. leaving out without explaining) much. Indeed, there has come to you from Allâh a light (guidance of Prophet Muhammad) and a plain Book (Qur'ân).*

Ma'aidah 5:19 O people of the Scripture (Jews and Christians)! Now has come to you Our Messenger (Muhammad) making (things) clear unto you, after a break in (the series of) Messengers, lest you say: "There came unto us no bringer of glad tidings and no Warner." But now has come unto you a bringer of glad tidings and a Warner. And Allâh is Able to do all things.

As I mentioned earlier, the Qur'an mentions Eesa (Jesus) with great honor and to believe in him (and all the prophets mentioned above) is an article of faith for the Muslim. Muslims believe that Jesus was one of the major prophets of Allah and this is one of the articles of faith without believing which a Muslim can't be a Muslim.

Allah clearly says that Eesa (Jesus) is His Messenger and the son of Maryam (Mary) born of immaculate conception and raised unto Allah and not crucified. Islam believes that it is for Allah to forgive whoever asks for forgiveness and that to do so He is not constrained to sacrifice someone who is innocent in the place of the one who committed the crime. Islam considers such an action to be highly unjust and against the justice of Allah.

So Eesa (Jesus) was not crucified but was saved from the Jews who wanted to crucify him and was raised up to Allah alive. Rasoolullah told us that one of the major signs of the approach of the Day of Judgment will be the return of Eesa (Jesus) to this world, where he will fight the Dajjal (what Christians call Anti-Christ) and kill him. He will declare himself to be a Muslim and will live a normal life, establish justice, marry and will die a natural death and will be buried. This is part of Muslim belief. Muslims believe in all of Eesa (Jesus) miracles, his immaculate conception, his life and message, his return before the Day of Judgment. Muslims do not believe him to be the son of God or God incarnate, they don't believe he was crucified and died and was resurrected but they believe that he was raised up alive and unharmed and will descend before the Day of Judgment.

It is interesting that in the oldest version of the Bible which has now been put online, there is no mention of the resurrection. The comment on the site says that, 'some familiar and very important passages are missing including the verses on resurrection.' I surmise that they are not missing but that they were never there because Jesus was not crucified or resurrected. These theories were later added when Jesus was deified and made Divine.

http://edition.cnn.com/2009/WORLD/europe/07/06/ancient.bible.online/index.html

It is time that our Christian brothers and sisters asked some deep and searching questions to their priests about what was done to the original Divine scripture that was revealed to Jesus and to Moses.

What is Jihad?

Jihad is the subject of much misconception thanks mostly to the lopsided reporting in the press and media which applies different rules to Muslims. For example when Black Africans, Indians and Colored People in South Africa carried on their armed struggle, guerilla warfare against the White Supremacy Apartheid regime for 50 years they were applauded and supported by the world which forced sanctions on the Apartheid Regime and forced it to abolish Apartheid and give freedom to the people of color.

However when Muslims fight occupation armies in Iraq, Afghanistan, Palestine, Chechnya and elsewhere who have made them refugees in their own lands and are randomly killing their women and children and taking over their homes, they are branded 'insurgents and terrorist'. Before giving any explanation of jihad it is essential that the world takes a close look at itself and its double standards with respect to Muslims.

Jihad (noun), Mujahada (verb) means 'struggle'. The Arabs use it for all kinds of struggles. For example someone may tell you that getting to office daily through the traffic is a great Mujahada (Jihad) for him. That does not mean that his office is in a foxhole on the battle front. Rasoolullahﷺ said that for the woman, Hajj is her jihad. That is because Hajj is a very strenuous activity and more so for the woman whose needs are different from those of men. So he gave it a special significance and reward for her. Similarly a Muslim may say about another that he does a lot of Mujahada in worship. That means that he spends a lot of time and goes to a lot of trouble of waking in the night to stand in Salah and fasting during the day and so on. None of these have anything to do with fighting or warfare.

The word for fighting/warfare is 'Qitaal' and has been used in the Qur'an in every place where fighting was indicated. The word 'Jihad' has been used in the above general meaning of struggling and working hard to achieve an objective and not for armed struggle or battle. This distinction is important to bear in mind as we'll see later.

The concept of 'Holy War' which is the way 'Qitaal' (which they call Jihad) is translated for English readers is a purely Christian concept relating to the Crusades which were declared to be a Holy War against the Infidels (Muslims). In Islam, war is not holy at all and strongly discouraged. War, like divorce, is seen as a necessary evil that must be avoided at all costs, but if there is no alternative then it may be engaged in, subject to all kinds of rules and regulations. Rasoolullahﷺ said about divorce, "It is the most hateful thing to Allahﷻ among the permitted things." So also with respect to war.

Allahﷻ permits people to defend themselves and to fight back but even to them he says that if they choose to forgive, it is better for them. For those who intend to oppress he warns them severely of punishment if they don't mend their ways.

He says:

Ash-Shura 42:40 The recompense for an evil is an evil like thereof, but whoever forgives and makes reconciliation, his reward is due from Allâh. Verily, He doesn't like the Zâlimûn (oppressors). **41.** *And indeed whosoever fights back after he has suffered wrong, for such there is no way (of blame) against them.***42.** *The way (of blame) is only against those who oppress men and wrongly rebel in the earth, for such there will be a painful torment.***43.** *And verily, whosoever shows patience and forgives that would truly be from the things recommended by Allâh.*

War with the object of colonizing people, stealing their resources, enslaving their populations, taking over their land and all such well accepted reasons for warfare are Haraam in Islam. Allah does not permit warfare for any of the above reasons and if any Muslim is waging war for any of these reasons, then that war is Haraam and is not jihad at all. It is strange or maybe not so strange if one looks at it closely, that the world does not criticize the colonial powers of old or the modern day for continuously waging war, economic, military, propaganda and societal on helpless nations who have no means to fight back. Once again speech with a forked tongue at its best.

It must be clear from the above that not every Qitaal (battle) is Jihad (religious or sanctioned by religion) and not every Jihad (struggle) is Qitaal (a battle). Having made that clear, let me reiterate that when Qitaal is done, it is subject to certain strict rules:

1. The only legal and permitted reason to take up arms in Islam is to establish justice and stop aggression and to defend Islam and Muslims. Muslims are also permitted to fight against aggression where they may not be the actual victims but are fighting to help others who are suffering. There is no blind support for Muslims in Islam. A Muslim is supposed to support whoever is right and to fight against whoever is wrong, irrespective of that person's religion, race or nationality.

Rasoolullahﷺ said, "Help your brother whether he is the aggressor or the victim." His Sahaba (Companions) asked him, "Ya Rasoolullahﷺ, we can understand if you say that we should help our brother if he is a victim of aggression. But you are saying that we should help him even if he is the aggressor. Can you please explain?" He replied, "Help him when he is the aggressor by standing up against him and stopping his aggression. Otherwise Allahﷻ will punish him far more severely in the Aakhira (Hereafter)."

Allahﷻ said:

Nisa 4:135 *O you who believe! Stand out firmly for justice, as witnesses to Allâh, even though it be against yourselves, or your parents, or your kin, be he rich or poor, Allâh is a Better Protector to both (than you). So follow not the lusts (of your hearts), lest you may avoid justice, and if you distort your witness or refuse to give it, verily, Allâh is Ever Well Acquainted with what you do*

2. Muslims however are permitted to defend their homes, families and property against aggressors and to fight with whatever means they have at their disposal. Not to permit someone to defend his own life, family or home would be the peak of injustice and Allahﷻ is not unjust. So Muslims are allowed to defend themselves if they are attacked.

3. Allahﷻ said:

   Ash-Shura 42:39 And those who, when an oppressive wrong is done to them, they fight back.
   Ash-Shura 41. And indeed whosoever fights back after he has suffered wrong, for such there is no way (of blame) against them.42. The way (of blame) is only against those who oppress men and wrongly rebel in the earth, for such there will be a painful torment.

4. A fully fledged Qitaal (armed struggle) in defense of Islam and Muslims can only be launched by the Imam of the Muslims, the Khalifa and not by any individual who feels aggrieved, no matter how justifiable his grievance may seem to him and his followers.

5. Muslims are permitted to join the army and fight in defense of their country even if the country is secular and not Muslim, because they are living in that country in peace and are able to practice their religion without hindrance. Such countries are called Dar-ul-Aman (Land of Peace).

6. Muslims are permitted to do all that they can to help others who are the victims of aggression and oppression irrespective of whether the victims are Muslim or not and irrespective of whether the aggressors are Muslim or not. For this Muslims are permitted to go and fight on the side of victims, wherever that may be.

7. In this fight however there are strict rules to be followed:

a. All non-combatants must be protected. So no blanket bombing is permitted. Special care must be taken to ensure that women and children are kept safely out of harm's way. Civilian population must be treated with kindness and respect and must not be abused in any way. None of their possessions or homes may be appropriated or occupied without payment. If they wish to leave the place they must be given safe passage and any assistance possible.

b. Livestock and standing crops, homes, hospitals, schools and places of public benefit must not be damaged. Drinking water must not be poisoned.

c. Places of worship (irrespective of religion) and priests and monks must not be harmed.

d. If a soldier surrenders he should be conveyed to a place of safety and must not be killed. His safety becomes the responsibility of the person he surrenders to and that person is answerable to Allahﷻ and to the chief of the Muslim army if he fails to protect the surrendered soldier.

e. If prisoners are taken, they must be treated with honor and may not be tortured or otherwise abused in any way. They must be properly fed, clothed and housed and if ransomed, must be released. If they are to be punished for war crimes, a proper investigation must be carried out and due process of law must be followed. Prisoners must be allowed to worship according to their beliefs and must not be forced to convert to Islam.

Allahﷻ says about prisoners of war:

Anfaal 8:70 *O Prophet! Say to the captives that are in your hands: "If Allâh knows any good in your hearts, He will give you something better than what has been taken from you, and He will forgive you, and Allâh is Oft-Forgiving, Most Merciful."*

In conclusion it may be noted that the canard spread about conversion by the sword is precisely that; a canard and a lie without any historical evidence to support it. It is not possible to convert anyone to any religion or ideology by force.

Belief is a matter of the heart and that is not subject to external force. People change their minds or religions because they see something good in the new way. That applies to all conversions, Christian, Buddhist, Muslim,

Republican, Democrat, Labor or Conservative. With respect to Islam we have historical evidence of entire countries embracing the new faith and remaining on it to this day, many centuries later.

The only country that left Islam after having a sizeable Muslim population is Spain and that was a direct result of the Inquisition and all its attendant tortures and burning at the stake anyone who did not recant and convert to Christianity. Other countries from Indonesia, China and Malaysia to India, the Middle East, Egypt, Syria and today large Muslim populations in Europe and America are all evidence that people convert to Islam because they like the religion. Not because anyone forced them. They key is to differentiate between propaganda and fact.

Hijab: Oppression or Liberation?

Today perhaps the most recognizable sign of the Muslim is the hijab of the Muslimah. The hijab has become a bone of contention, a symbol of self-confidence and a sign of assertiveness not just of the Muslim woman but of the entire Muslim Ummah. It is therefore necessary in my opinion to get all the facts right about the authority for this essential part of being a Muslim.

I would like to quote here a letter that a teenage girl wrote about her reasons for following the rules of hijab.

"I probably do not fit into the preconceived notion of a "rebel". I have no visible tattoos and minimal piercing. I do not possess a leather jacket. In fact, when most people look at me, their first thought usually is something along the lines of "oppressed female". The brave individuals who have mustered the courage to ask me about the way I dress usually have questions like: "Do your parents make you wear that?" or "Don't you find that really unfair?"

A while back, a couple of girls in Montreal were kicked out of school for dressing like I do. It seems strange that a little piece of cloth would make for such a controversy. Perhaps the fear is that I am harboring an Uzi machine gun underneath it! Of course, the issue at hand is more than a mere piece of cloth. I am a Muslim woman who, like millions of other Muslim women across the globe, chooses to wear a hijab. And the concept of the hijab, contrary to popular opinion, is actually one of the most fundamental aspects of female empowerment. When I cover myself, I make it virtually impossible for people to judge me according to the way I look. I cannot be categorized because of my attractiveness or lack thereof. Compare this to life in today's society: We are constantly sizing one another up on the basis of our clothing, jewelry, hair and makeup. What kind of depth can there be in a world like this?

Yes, I have a body, a physical manifestation upon this Earth. But it is the vessel of an intelligent mind and a strong spirit. It is not for the beholder to leer at or to use in advertisements to sell everything from beer to cars. Because of the superficiality of the world in which we live, external appearances are so stressed that the value of the individual counts for almost nothing. It is a myth that women in today's society are liberated. What kind of freedom can there be when a woman cannot walk down the street without every aspect of her physical self being "checked out"? When I wear the hijab I feel safe from all of this. I can rest assured that no one is looking at me and making assumptions about my character from the length of my skirt. There is a barrier between me and those who would exploit me.

I am first and foremost a human being; one of the saddest truths of our time is the question of the beauty myth and female self-image. Reading popular teenage magazines, you can instantly find out what kind of body image is "in" or "out". And if you have the "wrong" body type, well, then, you're just going to change it, aren't you? After all, there is no way you can be overweight and still be beautiful. Look at any advertisement. Is a woman being used to sell the product? How old is she? How attractive is she? What is she wearing? More often than not, that woman will be no older than her early 20s, taller, slimmer, and more attractive than average, and dressed in skimpy clothing. Why do we allow ourselves to be manipulated like this? Whether the 90s woman wishes to believe it or not, she is being forced into a mould. She is being coerced into selling herself, into compromising herself. This is why we have 13-year-old girls sticking their fingers down their throats to vomit and overweight adolescents hanging themselves.

When people ask me if I feel oppressed, I can honestly say no. I made this decision of my own free will. I like the fact that I am taking control of the way other people perceive me. I enjoy the fact that I don't give anyone anything to look at and that I have released myself from the bondage of the swinging pendulum of the fashion industry and other institutions that exploit females. My body is my own business. Nobody can tell me how I should look or whether or not I am beautiful. I know that there is more to me than that. I am also able to say no comfortably when people ask me if I feel as if my sexuality is being repressed. I have taken control of my sexuality. I am thankful I will never have to suffer the fate of trying to lose / gain weight or trying to find the exact lipstick shade that will go with my skin color. I have made choices about what my priorities are and these are not among them.

So next time you see me, don't look at me sympathetically. I am not under duress or a male-worshiping female captive from those barbarous Arab deserts. I've been liberated!

By Sultana Yusufali (a 17-year-old high school student)

Hijab is prescribed in Islam for women who have reached the age or puberty as a protection and distinction for them and so that they may be successful. Allahﷻ said:

Noor 24: 31. *And tell the believing women to lower their gaze (from looking at forbidden things), and protect their private parts (from illegal sexual acts, etc.) and not to show off their adornment except only that which is apparent (hands), and to draw their veils all over Juyubihinna (their bodies) and not to reveal their adornment except to their husbands, their fathers, their husband's fathers, their sons, their husband's sons, their brothers or their brother's sons, or their sister's sons, or their (Muslim) women (sisters in Islâm), or the (female) slaves whom their right hands possess, or old male servants who lack vigour, or small children who have no sense of the shame of sex. And let them not stamp their feet so as to reveal what they hide of their adornment. And all of you beg Allâh to forgive you all, O believers, that you may be successful.*

Allah is telling Muslim women that to stand out and be distinguished on the basis of something other than your outward appearance leads to success.

Allah also said that the hijab is protection for the woman from those who may be inclined to annoy her:

Al-Ahzab 33:59. *O Prophet! Tell your wives and your daughters and the women of the believers to draw their cloaks (veils) all over their bodies (screen themselves completely). That will be better, that they should be known (as free respectable women) so as not to be annoyed. And Allâh is Ever Oft Forgiving, Most Merciful*

The entire Western charade of women's independence is a farce. Very cleverly done by a society dominated by men whose only interest lies in exploiting women and using them as playthings. So they have convinced the women of their society, that their "freedom and empowerment" lies in showing their bodies to the world. But tell me seriously, who is it that wants to see a bare female body more - a man or a woman? So who "benefits" when a woman puts her beauty and sex on show? Now why is that so difficult to understand? Ask yourself why if women are so free and empowered in the West, there are not more than 3 women CEOs of American corporations? Ask yourself why even the idea of a President as a woman is unthinkable in the US after 200 years of existence?

As a result they have created a society where the first 13 years of her life, a girl's constant concern is whether or not she will be able to get a boy to escort her to the Prom when they graduate from high school. So high school education is less about getting knowledge than about finding and hanging on to a boyfriend, long enough for him to take her to the Prom. Then comes Prom night which has the highest rate of teenage suicides (all the poor dumb idiots who did not get a boyfriend) and the highest rate of teenage pregnancies (payment for taking her to the Prom). Ask yourself, what are you seeing here? Women's emancipation or women's slavery? Who is in charge? The man or the woman?

Islam emancipates the woman. Sets her free from the yoke of having to please every man in her environment by being attractive to him and "giving in" to him in one way or the other. It gives women respect in that nobody has the right to demand that they should show their bodies. It gives them the freedom to be respected on the basis of their competence, knowledge, wisdom and capability; not only on account of their sex appeal to those who have no right to be concerned about their sex appeal.

What are the rights of women in Islam?

Islam gives rights to women which in many societies are amazing even today. Imagine the effect of these rights in 5th century Arabia or in Europe when Muslims went there less than 100 years later. Women were property to be used and discarded at will. Islam said that they are individuals with rights and privileges. Islam raised the honor of the mother and said that Jannah (Paradise) lies under her feet. Islam prohibited female infanticide which was common in Arabia at that time and which is still common in India 14 centuries later.

Islam gives the woman the right to inherit and hold property. It gives her the right to earn an income, to possess wealth and to dispose of it as she wills without needing to take anyone's permission. It gives her the right to marry whoever she wishes as long as he is Muslim and to refuse any suitor without giving any reason. It gives her the right to divorce her husband. It gives the widow and divorcee to remarry.

When she marries neither she nor her family need to spend any money. It is the man who comes to her with gifts and marries her after paying the Mehr (dower or wedding gift). If he divorces her, he forgoes that amount, all the gifts, jewelry or property that he may have given her until then and has to give her an allowance to maintain herself until she marries again or until any children she has from that marriage are old enough to support her. All she earns, inherits or receives as gifts is hers alone. She has no responsibility or compulsion to share it with her husband or to put it into the family pool. The woman has no compulsion to serve her husband's parents or family and even has the right to demand an allowance to breast feed her own children. All these are her legal rights, enforceable in a court of law in the Islamic State. That is why I said that even to this day, these rights are revolutionary in nature.

What is Islamic Fundamentalism – Is it fact or fiction?

We are no strangers to reports of 'Islamic Terrorism' or 'Fundamentalism' in Islam. The important thing is for us to see in perspective, whether the terrorism that we see is indeed 'Islamic' or it is forbidden in Islam, no matter what its perpetrators claim. It is indeed unfortunate that when a terrorist group commits an act and says it is doing it in the name of Islam, the world is so eager to believe it. But when genocide is committed in Bosnia by Christians or in Bombay by Hindus or in the Occupied Territories by the Jews, nobody denounces those religions. The fact is that no religion espouses killing of innocent people. We all know this. But still we believe what we read, knowing what we do.

To quote John Esposito, who is an advisor to the US Government on Islamic affairs, in his book, 'The Islamic Threat': *"Much of the reassertion of religion in politics and society has been subsumed under the term 'Islamic fundamentalism'. Although 'fundamentalism' is a common designation, in the press and increasingly among academics it is used in a variety of ways. For a number of reasons, it tells us everything and yet nothing. First, all those who call for a return to foundational beliefs or the 'fundamentals' of a religion may be called fundamentalist. In a strict sense this could include all practicing Muslims, who accept the Qur'an as the literal word of God and the*

Sunnah (example) of the Prophet Muhammad as a normative model for living. Second, our understanding and perceptions of fundamentalism are heavily influenced by American Protestantism. Webster's Ninth New Collegiate Dictionary defines the term fundamentalism - as a "movement in the 20th century Protestantism emphasizing the literally interpreted Bible as fundamental to Christian life and teaching." For many liberal or mainline Christians, "fundamentalist" is pejorative and derogatory, being applied rather indiscriminately to all those who advocate a literalist biblical position and thus are regarded as static, retrogressive and extremist. As a result, fundamentalism often has been regarded popularly as referring to those who are literalists and wish to return to and replicate the past. In fact, few individuals or organizations in the Middle East fit such a stereotype. Indeed, many fundamentalist leaders have had the best education, enjoy responsible positions in society and create viable modern institutions such as schools, hospitals, and social service agencies".

This last statement is if anything, even more true of the Muslims in the US and in India. However this is a fact, which is often downplayed and never highlighted, when making blanket statements covering all of us. India has been home to Muslims for the past 1400 years, give or take a decade or two, when the first Muslim traders landed in Kodangallur in Kerala.

The local king Cheranan Perumal welcomed them, gave them land to settle and construct a masjid which exists and is active to this day and later accepted Islam himself. He then undertook a journey to Madina in Arabia to meet the Prophet but died enroute in Salalah in Oman, where he is buried. Muslims are people who have contributed to every aspect of Indian society and culture and whose signs and impact are proudly visible and displayed to this day. After all it is the Taj Mahal which is the best recognized symbol of

India and the ramparts of the Red Fort that the Prime Minister addresses the nation from. It is true that bad news sells better than good news, but can sale considerations justify vilifying an entire community and extracting the periodic price of citizenship in blood and lives that has been the lot of the Indian Muslim? And the pogroms go on, blatantly and openly, as happened in Bombay and Gujarat and elsewhere the perpetrators of which walk free to this day while the surviving victims live in refugee camps in their own cities, driven from their homes and made destitute overnight for no reason other than that they worshipped Allahﷻ.

In the US and Europe today, we are seeing a growing trend of anti-Muslim feeling. Not because the Muslims who live in that country have done anything to deserve it, but because the press makes money speculating on vague rumors and does not care about the problems this creates for people who want to follow Islam. For example, a friend of mine was praying the evening prayer in a parking lot on the Boston Turnpike one day when a man drove his car right up to him (almost as if to run him down), then got out and asked in a loud voice, "Tell me something, why do you Arabs hate us so much?" As it happened, he turned out to be a very reasonable fellow (he was an attorney) when my friend asked him if he believed everything he read in the papers or heard on talk shows. And was quite embarrassed when my friend pointed out to him the assumptions he was making, including that he was Arab.

Esposito goes on to say, *"I regard 'fundamentalism as too laden with Christian presuppositions and Western stereotypes, as well as implying a monolithic threat that does not exist; more fitting general terms are "Islamic Revivalism" or "Islamic Activism", which are less value-laden and have roots within the Islamic tradition. Islam possesses a long tradition of revival (tajdid) and reform (islah) which includes notions of political and social activism dating from early Islamic centuries to the present day."*

As a result, the stereotype of some kind of monolithic Islamic threat is raised. Muslims have contributed to and continue to contribute to every aspect of society. Yet that contribution is neither acknowledged nor appreciated. Instead, strident calls are raised against 'Muslim invaders'. The same standard is for example, not applied to the British who actually subjugated and enslaved half the world for centuries and systematically exploited it and destroyed local industry and enterprise.

This attitude also means that we never learn the lessons that history is replete with. The consequence is mutual distrust and suspicion, which has been the legacy of Muslim-Christian relations in the West. When you put all these together we have a situation where a Hindu who goes to the temple or does his daily pooja, or a Church going Christian is not called fundamentalist but a Muslim who prays regularly is.

The term 'Islamic Terrorism' has been created apparently with the purpose of creating a global fantasy of the world being in danger from some kind of Islamic domination. The negative experience that Western society had with clubbing the Church and temporal rule together and the negative way in which the Church reacted to scientific discoveries (e.g. Galileo and many others were persecuted for saying that the earth was not the center of the universe) led to the separation of the Church from politics in most Western countries. However this experience is applied indiscriminately to the Islamic world, which never had the same problems and demands are made that the Muslims also separate their religion from their temporal affairs. Little attention is paid to the fact that Islam guides both religious and temporal and that it is therefore impossible for a Muslim who practices Islam to separate one from the other.

Muhammadﷺ was always open to learning and Islam is a complete way of life, not a set of worship related rituals. The Qur'an 1430 years ago spoke of genetic codes, embryonic development, all life arising from water, galaxies and planets with the earth being only one of them, and many such facts which the Western world only accepted many centuries later. There has never been a religion versus science divide in Islam.

Yet Islam is sought to be showcased as a backward religion, unfit to be followed in the modern world. Sadly, our own lack of knowledge about our religion and the Qur'an creates a sense of apology in us, instead of the pride, which our Islam warrants. One of the most famous sayings of the Prophet Muhammadﷺ is that the acquisition of knowledge is obligatory on a Muslim.

Islam consequently prescribes a political system, a personal law code and a way to worship God, all in one, something that the Western mind seems incapable of accepting. Consequently, when Muslims who practice Islam and who also talk of living their lives or of running their countries in the Islamic way are termed "fundamentalist".

To quote Esposito again, *"Focus on "Islamic fundamentalism" as a global threat has reinforced a tendency to equate violence with Islam, to fail to distinguish between illegitimate use of religion by individuals and the faith and practice of the majority of the world's Muslims who, like believers in other religious traditions, wish to live in peace. To uncritically equate Islam and Islamic fundamentalism with extremism is to judge Islam only by those who wreak havoc, a standard not applied to Judaism and Christianity. Fear of fundamentalism creates a climate in which Muslims and Islamic organizations are guilty until proven innocent. Actions, however heinous, are attributed to Islam rather than to a twisted or distorted interpretation of Islam. Thus, for example, despite the historic track record of Christianity and Western countries in conducting warfare, developing weapons of mass destruction, and imposing their imperialist designs, Islam and Muslim culture are portrayed as somehow peculiarly and inherently expansionist and prone to violence and warfare (jihad). The risk today is that exaggerated fears will lead to double standards in promotion of democracy and human rights in the Muslim world. Witness the volume of Western democratic concern and action for the former Soviet Union and Eastern Europe but muted or ineffective response with regard to the promotion of democracy in the Middle East or the defense of Muslims in Bosnia-Herzegovinia and Chechnya".*

The West has very successfully propagated the myth of Christianity and the West, being peaceful and focused to creating harmony. One only has to read the history of the people in Africa, Asia, and South America who were killed, sold into slavery and subjugated in the most inhuman and cruel ways to understand how big a scam this is. Unfortunately, with English language being the medium of education; being educated often means being able to speak English. One of the spin-offs of this is a distorted vision of history, which paints the history of the Western imperialist people in a favorable light while maligning everyone else. The most maligned in this are Islam and Muslims as they were for many years the only serious threat to Western imperialism.

Witness the Crusades (which the Europeans lost) or the presence of the Ottoman Empire at the gateway to the East, which prevented the Europeans from entering Asia for several centuries. The fall of the Ottomans heralded the slavery of Asia (India, China, Japan) for two centuries and a systematic despoiling of one country for the enrichment of another.

Islam is a religion that is followed by 1.6 billion people in the world living in 52 Muslim countries and that does not include India, which has a population of 200 million Muslims. To malign this great religion primarily due to the doings of a few people (whose actions are neither Islamic nor human, no matter what they may claim) through misrepresented and deliberately distorted press reporting has unfortunately become the norm. The normal citizen can't stop anyone making these claims. But we can certainly stop believing them. For example, when a Middle Eastern group indulges in terrorist activity, the press calls them Islamic terrorists. But when the IRA does the same action, they don't call them Roman Catholic or Christian terrorists. Or when the Eastern Orthodox Christians in Kosovo massacre their Muslim neighbors and rape their women, the press says they are engaging in 'ethnic cleansing' and conveniently forgets to mention their religion. Neither does it print pictures of the Pope or St. Paul's Cathedral to reinforce the image of the religion of the criminals.

We don't have to look too far back in the history of reporting in America to find instances where, when a youth of African-American origin committed any crime, his ethnicity was reported before his identity ("Black man commits felony"). Yet does anyone remember the KKK as being called "Christian?" Thankfully, this is not done any more as we have been able to realize the cumulative effect of this where even today, America sends more black men to jail than it sends to college. What a colossal waste of human resource? When we can see how harmful this has been for America, why can't we see how harmful the discrimination against Muslims is likely to be for the world?

Why is it so difficult to understand that discrimination against anyone is harmful for everyone, including the one that is doing the discrimination. When will we learn this lesson? And at what cost? It is a matter of the greatest concern; that we learn to look at the reality and not get carried away by propaganda. I believe that we are moving towards a time where people are not going to allow anyone to lead them un-protesting towards slaughter in the name of ethnic cleansing.

And neither can we live behind high fortress walls like the feudal lords of Europe did, during the Dark Ages.

The future of this world of ours lies only in international understanding, mutual respect and the complete destruction of all discrimination against any people, irrespective of their religion or ethnicity or nationality. We have two alternatives. Either we work to wipe out the conditioning of which all of us, alike are victims, and work towards promoting understanding between people, irrespective of religious belief. Or we prepare ourselves for civil war and universal suffering of a magnitude that I dare not imagine. No matter what anyone tells us, 1.4 billion Muslims are not going to vanish, just because some people don't like their presence.

And even if they do, then who will be next on that list of vanishing people, I wonder.

What is Sufism and what is its connection with Islam?

The word 'Sufism' interestingly is a British-English coinage. In Islamic theology or literature it doesn't exist in this form. An 'ism' is a religion or a complete ideology, religious or otherwise; for example, Hinduism, Communism and so on. However you wouldn't call the Bhakti movement in Hinduism as 'Bhaktisim', would you? That is because it is not a distinct and different religion or theology in itself but an approach to Hindu theology.

Islam recognizes a four step process to connecting with Allahﷻ. Being informed (reading) about the Word of Allahﷻ; purifying oneself (internal and external); understanding the Word and implementing it in your life (Sunnah – the way of Muhammadﷺ).

One of these four essential steps is purification, called Tazkiya in Arabic. This consists of purifying the body, clothes and surroundings as well as (and very importantly) purifying the heart (self) from all negative emotions like arrogance, greed, hatred, envy, jealousy, anger, lust, fear and so on. Islam teaches us that knowledge of Allahﷻ and a connection with Him can only be built if the heart is purified of all negativity and this is reflected in a person's actions. So therefore, Tazkiya consists of not only purifying the heart but of demonstrating this to oneself (and one's spiritual guide) through a change in behavior, actions and decisions. Rasoolullahﷺ trained his companions in this way and so did all those teachers who came after him.

When Islam spread from Arabia into Iran and then into India, it encountered several philosophies. It met the mythologies and concepts of Gods of the Greeks, in Egypt it met the Coptic Christians with their practices of monasticism and self-denial in pursuit of spiritual awakening. In Iran and India, Muslims encountered Zoroastrianism of the Persians and the Aryan religions of India, Hinduism, Buddhism and Jainism The principal difference between these religious philosophies and Islam and indeed all the revelation based religions like Christianity and Judaism was the special place given to God. In all the revelation based religions, Allahﷻ is considered completely separate from and above, all creation. Even in Christianity where they elevated Isa (Jesus) to the position of Son of God, they still have God (the Father) as a separate entity.

In the Aryan philosophies however they had confused the Creator with His creatures and had conceptualized that since the Creator existed before all creation, the creatures must necessarily have come from Him and so are in fact parts of, or the manifestation of the Creator. So they had the concept of Avatars and it became acceptable to worship any object in creation since it was in any case a reflection, or manifestation of the personality of the Creator. That is also how the concept of transmigration of soul and rebirth came about. The theory then was that if one did not lead a good life then they would be sent back again and again (sometimes in the form of other creatures) until they 'paid the price' of their sins. The final goal of life was to become one with the Creator.

When Islam came into these lands, the truth that it brought in the form of the actual speech of the Creator (The Qur'an) in which He introduced Himself and told mankind who He is and what their relationship to Him is; the concept was so totally at odds with these philosophies that some of the Muslims allowed themselves to get confused. So they invented the theory of Wahdat-al-Wujood (Unity of Existence) in a needless attempt to 'bridge the gap' between pure Islamic Monotheism and Hindu and Buddhist philosophies.

This theory basically says the same thing as the Hindu philosophy of Advaith: that there is only one being and that is God. All creation is from His person and so He is actually inside all things and everywhere. And that the ultimate aim of a person is to live such a life that one day that person becomes one with Allahﷻ and can actually say, An-allah (I am Allah). People like Al Hallaj, Sufi Sarmast are reported to have said this. Bayazid Bistami is supposed to have made statements like, "Subhanee (All praise to me)" and "There is nothing inside this cloak except Allah", and other similar statements. All such statements are Kufr and apostasy in Islam.

The kindest thing that can be said about them is that if they were spoken by the person in a state of involuntary spiritual intoxication, then they must be ignored as he has lost control of his senses and so anything he says is immaterial and not a sign of anything other than temporary madness.

If on the other hand he said these in a state of intoxication that was deliberately induced by using drugs, alcohol or music and dancing, then he is guilty of two major sins; the intoxication and the Kufr (apostasy) that he spoke. The propounders of this philosophy of Wahdat-al-Wujood forget the fact that this philosophy has no basis in Islam and in the sources of Islam, i.e. the Qur'an and Sunnah.

Therefore some so-called Sufis refuse to pray in the formal Islamic way, Salah, and smoke marijuana, sing 'devotional' songs which claim for man the status of demigod and dance in a state of drug induced 'ecstasy', claiming that the rules for ordinary people are different from the rule for the 'Friends' of Allahﷻ - as they claim themselves to be. Rasoolullahﷺ himself did not make such a claim for himself or his family, yet these people claim such things and the ignorant believe them and call them 'saints'. They acquired a 'divine' status with ignorant disciples. When they died their disciples and others ignorant of the basic beliefs of Islam started to worship at their graves and to ask them for favors and claimed that they can intercede with Allahﷻ on their behalf. All these practices, in Islam, amount to polytheism and are the antithesis of Islamic Monotheism. Islam doesn't recognize any saints – this is a Christian concept – because in Islam all people are equal and anyone can reach Allahﷻ provided he follows the correct path as shown by Muhammadﷺ and not something invented by anyone else. Every human being has access to Allahﷻ and doesn't need anyone special to intercede for him. Islam doesn't recognize that the dead can do anything for the living, no matter who the dead person is. And it specifically prohibits worshiping anyone other than Allahﷻ, living or dead.

The so-called 'Sufis' however claimed that man is created from four elements: fire, water, earth and air; which is the essence of Hindu philosophy of creation and directly against the Ayaat of the Qur'an where Allahﷻ clearly stated that He created the first prototype of man from clay and created the system of his procreation by means of seminal fluid. (Qur'an 32:7-9) Allahﷻ also stated clearly that He created the Jinn from fire. (Qur'an 55:14-15) There is no combination of elements mentioned anywhere in the Qur'an and those who make these claims took them from Hindu philosophy when Islam came into contact with Hinduism in India.

Later as time passed, these graves (Dargah, Maqaam) became a source of huge income for their caretakers as devotees left offerings and money. Song and dance became a part of the rituals of these places. The celebration of the birthday (Urs) and death day of the so-called 'saint' became major religious events and festivals, attracting yet more income for the caretakers. Rituals were adopted from the rituals of Hindu temples – washing of the grave with 'blessed' water and milk, smearing it with sandalwood paste, clothing it with an embroidered cover, making circumambulations of it, breaking coconuts, lighting candles and lamps and making supplications to the grave in the belief that they will be answered. All these which came into

Islam in India are an exact replication of rituals at Hindu temples. Some misguided Sufis encouraged various local cultural practices which were prevalent in India in order to make Islam more user friendly and acceptable to a polytheistic people.

This was a major mistake as it took away the differentiator of Islam and undermined its most basic and fundamental theology of monotheism. In the same way, the Sufis also encouraged singing and music, especially the singing of devotional songs, called Qawwali which are designed to send the listener into a state of 'ecstasy'.

A good example of this is **Ab'ul Hasan Yamīn ud-Dīn Khusrow** (1253-1325 CE) better known as **Amīr Khusrow (also Khusrau, Khusro) Dehlawī** who was an iconic figure in the cultural history of the Indian subcontinent. Amir Khusrow was a spiritual disciple of Nizamuddin Auliya of Delhi and was a notable poet and a prolific and seminal musician. He wrote poetry primarily in Persian, but also in Hindavi. He is regarded as the *"father of Qawwali"* (the devotional music of the Sufis in the Indian subcontinent). He is also credited with enriching Hindustani classical music by introducing Persian and Arabic elements in it, and was the originator of the Khayal and Tarana styles of music. The invention of the Tabla and Sitar is also traditionally attributed to Amīr Khusrow.

A musician and a scholar, Amir Khusrow was as prolific in tender lyrics as in highly involved prose and could easily emulate all styles of Persian poetry. The verse forms he wrote include Ghazal, Masnavi, Qata, Rubai and Tarkibhand. His contribution to the development of the *Ghazal*, hitherto little used in India, is particularly significant. Qawwali has developed into a major art form and is a significant part of Indian classical music and has had many famous performers through the ages.

However none of this is Islam. And that is the problem. One can't claim to attain to spiritual station in any religion by going out of that religion. One may well be inventing his own religion but can't at the same time claim to any station of spiritual attainment in the religion that one left. That is exactly what happened to the so-called Sufis who introduced polytheistic and other practices into Islam. They invented another religion which is not Islam and consequently left Islam themselves – even though they don't accept this and claim to high spiritual rank within Islam. However it is for Allah ﷻ to judge and He will no doubt do so. But if one were to use simple logic and ask, 'What is the Islam that Muhammad ﷺ brought?' And, 'How does this new Sufi version compare with the original template?' The answers would be clear enough. It doesn't compare at all. It is something else. It is not Islam; the Islam of Muhammad ﷺ and his Companions.

Sufis also started to indulge in all sorts of special rituals of worship and invented practices and theories to support them and taught these to their special initiates. These developed into what came to be known as Tareeqa (The

Way) and a parallel theology was created to the Shari'ah (Law) of Islam, called the Tareeqat (The Way). The Sufis claimed that this was a higher state of being and awareness and was not subject to the Shari'ah, which they claimed was for ordinary mortals and so many of their leaders didn't follow the foundational principles of the Shari'ah. This is the origin of what came to be called 'Sufism', which became a religion in itself. However as I said, this is not Islam.

The fact that all their practices were antithetical to Islam mattered little to these Sufis who practiced their own version of what they called Islam which lost all resemblance to the pure Monotheistic truth that Muhammad ﷺ came with.

As I mentioned earlier, there is a very significant place in Islam for spiritual development and the way to do that is through purification of one's life – both internal and external. However that is hard work and people prefer to live in a fantasy and believe the false claims of the 'Sufis' that singing and dancing and blind obedience to their 'Shaikh' and generously keeping him supplied with the wherewithal to maintain his lifestyle is sufficient to attain the highest stations with Allah ﷻ and Jannah in the Aakhira.

However reality is not dependent on belief. So whatever the Sufis and their disciples may like to believe, there is no running away from the fact that unless one believes in and practices pure monotheism as taught by the Messenger of Allah ﷻ, Muhammad ﷺ, there will be no deliverance on the

Day of Judgment and all practitioners of polytheistic philosophies will find themselves together, in trouble.

It is good to remember that Islam does not recognize the philosophy that there are many ways to Allahﷻ. If that was so, then there would be no point in sending a Messenger with a message. People could be left to themselves to approach Allahﷻ in any way they liked. However that is not what Allahﷻ did. He sent His Word and His Messengerﷺ to explain the Word and to demonstrate how it is to be lived in practice. He said clearly that on the Day of Judgment, no religion other than Islam would be accepted and that the only religion which He recognizes is Islam. Whether we like it or not, if we believe that the Qur'an is the Word of Allahﷻ, His Speech, then we must believe what He told us. He said:

Ma'aida 3: 85. *And whoever seeks a religion other than Islam, it will never be accepted of him, and in the Hereafter he will be one of the losers.*

Ma'aida 3: 19. *Truly, the religion with Allah is Islam. Those who were given the Scripture (Jews and Christians) did not differ except, out of mutual jealousy, after knowledge had come to them. And whoever disbelieves in the Ayat (revelation) of Allah, then surely, Allah is Swift in calling to account.*

Islam invites to fact, the truth as revealed by the Creator who sees, hears and knows everything visible and hidden. It speaks with the authority of absolute knowledge without any doubt. The Qur'an is the actual speech of Allahﷻ and this is clear from its tone of majestic command. It is not for nothing that many of the greatest linguists of Arabia bowed before Allah﷾ because they recognized His speech and declared that what they were hearing when Muhammadﷺ recited it, was not the word of man.

Islam is a unique religion which to this day is the only one which makes this claim, that it is directly from Allah﷾ and supports this claim by means of scientific evidence which shows that the claim is irrefutable.

With this, we invite the reader to the universal brotherhood of Islam; to connect with his or her Creator and become one of those who will be saved on the Day when nothing else can save them.

Conclusion

I hope that this little book will pave the way for frank and open discussion leading to understanding between people. It is only when we accept each other's differences and genuinely seek to understand without sitting in judgment, that we build bonds that cross boundaries of all kinds.

I am sure you will agree that to build such bonds and to cross barriers is a critical need today.

I live by my principle: I will not allow what is not in my control to prevent me from doing what is in my control.

So this book.

Mirza Yawar Baig

www.yawarbaig.org

Notification: Anyone who would like to print/publish this book may do so on condition that it is not sold commercially and that no changes are made in it.

Mirza Yawar Baig

Founder of **YAWAR BAIG & ASSOCIATES**™. International Speaker, Author, Life Coach, Trainer, Corporate Consultant, specializing in Leadership Development helping technical specialists transition into Management and Leadership roles. He helps Family Businesses make the critical transition from being 'Person-led to becoming Process-driven' and create robust systems that will enable the business to be handed from generation to generation. Yawar's book, **'The Business of Family Business'** shows business families how to grow, yet stay together. Yawar is a life coach and mentor for prominent family businesses in India, South Africa & Sri Lanka. Yawar specializes in helping Start-ups make the transition into their growth phase, helping them to look at challenges and take difficult critical decisions. In 27 years of training and consulting Yawar has taught more than 200,000 managers, administrators, teachers, technologists and clergy on 3 continents.

His other publications include:

- The Business of Family Business
- Hiring Winners
- Present Your Way to the Top
- A Journey of Faith

www.yawarbaig.com   yawarbaig@gmail.com